Professionals reporting good results with TPM

For the first time in my 20 year career as a clinical social worker, I am witnessing lasting miraculous healing by the Lord Jesus Christ in the trauma memories of my clients. I see patients (who before, I did not believe were even emotionally strong enough by clinical standards), move towards memory work and find resolution of their trauma and become high functioning members of society because of what Jesus' is doing through Theophostic Prayer Ministry. **Dr. James W. Eisenhower, Licensed Clinical Social Worker.**

As executive director of a faith-based transitional housing/recovery program, I view the Theophostic Prayer method as a critical part of the recovery program. We minister primarily to people with drug and alcohol addictions. When designing our program we knew our success would be based on whether or not the program residents were truly set free from the bondage of drugs and alcohol. Knowing that these addictions are the surface issues of deeper problems, Theophostic ministry helps us get to those root causes. **Larry Refsland, Executive Director, Rewind, Inc.**

I had worked as a mental health professional for 25 years before I was introduced to Theophostic Ministries in January of 2002. As a Christian counselor I had tried every major secular and Christian counseling approach and I was getting "tolerable recovery" and as the director of a sex offender treatment program, I was getting "intolerable recovery" with the clients. For this reason, I was excited when I first heard about TPM and after almost 3 years of using TPM I am still excited. It has truly revolutionized my life and my practice. I am now in private practice and doing some work for a Christian Youth Home that hired me to train their staff to do TPM. One boy who was admitted to our facility was in deep pain when he arrived because his best friend had been killed 2 weeks earlier. I prayed with him using this approach and he was set free from the pain and grief of that loss in the first session. He has since received Jesus as his Savior and is continuing to receive healing in other areas of his life. I am thankful that God has shown me how He can heal people through the use of these simple biblical principles. **Jim Gardner, Ph.D. Nashville**

I am a Clinical Social Worker with a private practice. I have been counseling for about seven years and had gotten to the spot of frustration and questioning my career choice. I have been using Theophostic Ministry for about a year. The most memorable case, beside my own, is a client I had worked with for two years. She is very young and had lost her husband in a horseback riding accident. The grieving process has been long and hard, but in a Theophostic moment God revealed to her a scene of such utter peace and tranquility that she stated, "I will never feel alone again." Her life has turned around in a dramatic way, proving God wants His children to be set free. I pray that I will continue to be available to God to use me to help others discover the truth they need to be free indeed. **Vickie Knowlden, LCSW professional counselor in private practice.**

As a mental health professional with 25 years of counseling experience, I never cease to be amazed with the effectiveness of Theophostic Prayer Ministry in my practice. I have used this method for many thousands of hours over the last five years and routinely witness God working directly, powerfully and consistently to restore emotionally wounded people's lives. Without wanting to sound flippant, the miraculous has become common-place. But then the miraculous is normal and common for God. **Frank Meadows, professional counselor in private practice.**

We have been applying the Theophostic Principles for five years at "Recovery for the City", a faith-based 12 step program for people who seeking freedom from addictions and compulsive behaviors. Many hundreds of people have found true freedom as they have invited the Risen Lord Jesus Christ into the places of their deepest hurts. We especially see Jesus showing up when people release their bitterness and sinful past as they embrace Him as their personal Lord and Savior. What an approach to Evangelism! Who would not want to give their lives to The One who can, not only forgive sins, but also heal the broken heart!" Gary accepted Christ in my office and was healed of the abuses his dad had produced in his life. He had not been sober in his adult life. Today, he's been sober for three years and is one of our leaders. **Dr. Paul Hardy, founder of "Recovery for the City", Virginia Beach**

We are a five-year-old center for healing prayer. Three years ago, we begin to use Theophostic prayer and now we have 25 weekly prayer volunteer and we are still booked two months in advance for Theophostic prayer. We have seen hundreds of people set free! **Rev. Kathy Eason, Director, Serenity Retreat for Healing and Spiritual Renewal, Houston**

I am a chaplain for Hospice. When many of my clients or their loved ones are very sick, they begin to feel the weight of their past decisions. Some feel guilt, helplessness, or fear. Because of Theophostic Prayer Ministry, they have been able to go back to the source and origin of their feelings. They have forgiven their family members. Jesus has come and healed them, enabling them to face intense transitions with peace. They become confident as they realize Jesus is there with them and that He cares enough to gently heal them. **Virginia Norris**

Prior to using Theophostic Prayer Ministry, I had practiced psychotherapy with marginal success for 21 years from a secular, cognitive-behavioral approach in counseling. This secular approach changed completely when I received training in Theophostic Prayer Ministry. I have completed all training that this ministry offers to include the Basic and Advanced training and both the Level I and Level II Apprenticeship. My role as psychotherapist has shifted from being in control to leading the client to Jesus. The paradigm shift has taken effort and commitment, but I am delighted to look to Jesus for understanding and direction. The effectiveness of the approach is confirmed by the marvelous healing (mind renewal) I continually witness in people that Christ provides when TPM is offered. These results are being confirmed by a two-year research project in which I participated, that is promising statistically significant spiritual, mental and behavioral transformation in over 80% of the cases we studied. Clients consistently report deep inner healing and a realization of truth and resultant life transformation as I administer this process. It is both awesome and humbling and I am grateful to the Lord for this powerful and effective way of providing healing. I believe that every person involved in professional or lay ministry will benefit from each of these training experiences as well. **Dr. Terry Zuehlke, private practice.**

Theophostic Prayer Ministry has proven an effective therapeutic tool with selected patients in the psychiatric hospital environment. Not only has this emotional healing tool made a significant difference in treatment outcome in the lives of most patients involved, but also its effects have been most meaningful in my personal life. **Richard L. Bowen, M.Div., Th.M., L.C.S.W. Clinical Chaplain.**

Finally, a divinely powerful counseling method pastors can confidently use in church ministry. I am watching person after person truly find freedom and release from the pain God never intended for them to carry. **Rev. Dwaine Tilford, Pastor.**

Theophostic Prayer Ministry has not only changed my ministry and the way I do counseling as a pastor, but has truly changed my life... Every pastoral counselor needs this training without exception! **Jeffery Eaton, Pastor.**

TPM has revolutionized my Christian Counseling practice since I began employing it in 2001. When I simply get out of the way, and let God take over the session, and follow TPM exactly as I am trained, my clients experience breakthroughs that are nothing short of miraculous. (And I do not use that word lightly). Moreover, these breakthroughs take place in a matter of a few short hours in most cases. The results, as far as I can see in follow-ups, are permanent: Anger, depression, and anxiety are replaced by love, joy, and peace, which is exactly what we should expect when our wounds are brought into the presence of God (Gal 5:22). I firmly believe that TPM will be remembered as a great turning point in the history of emotional and psychological healing, and it is very exciting to be a part of what God is doing. **Scott Lownsdale, Ed.D. Licensed Clinical Professional Counselor.**

Healing Life's Hurts

Through Theophostic Prayer

Edward M. Smith

New Creation Publishing
2002, 2005

Published by New Creation Publishing

Printed in the U.S.A.

For additional information and ordering other Theophostic Prayer Ministry training materials call 1-270-465-3757 or visit www.theophostic.com

Originally co-published by Servant Publications and New Creation Publishing Inc. in 2002.

Contents

Author's Statement of Faith

I believe that . . .

• There is one God, eternally coexistent in three persons: the Father, the Son and the Holy Spirit. The Father sent His only Son to become the redemption for lost mankind. The Holy Spirit was sent to complete the mission of Christ through His body, the Church.

• The Bible is the inspired Word of God and is "profitable for teaching, reproof, correction and training in righteousness" (2 Tim. 3:16). It is timeless and relevant for all circumstances and is the fullness of God's divine inspired revelation to man, without error in its original form.

• Jesus Christ came in the flesh fully God and fully man, yet without sin. As God the Son, He came to earth as a man, born of a virgin, fulfilled all He was sent to accomplish, died on the cross for the sins of the world, after three days rose from the dead and rules today at the right hand of God the Father. He will return in the clouds on the day appointed by the Father to call up all those who belong to Him who have been regenerated by the atoning work of the cross of Christ. Jesus Christ is central to all true renewal and freedom. Apart from Him we can do nothing (see John 15:5).

• The Holy Spirit is the third person of the Trinity. He lives within the heart of the true Christian, providing the power to obey God's Word, convicting of sin, teaching and leading into all truth, providing comfort in time of distress and unifying all true believers in a bond of love. The Holy Spirit is the way that God communicates with His people through opening up the written Word and through inner communication of the heart.

• The Church is universally made up of all people who believe Jesus Christ died on the cross for their sins and rose from the dead by the power of the Heavenly Father, and through faith become partakers of the divine nature. The indwelling of the Spirit of Christ is the determining factor of one's authentic faith relationship with God, not one's denomination, religious practice or performance in Christian disciplines. For "if anyone does not have the Spirit of Christ, he does not belong to Him" (Rom. 8:9).

• The primary call and mission of the Church is to go forth and proclaim the good news of freedom in Christ to all the world (see Matt. 28:19-20), to bring truth to those held captive by the grip of the kingdom of darkness, and to prepare the way for His second coming by making ready His bride (see Luke 4:18).

• All people are born with a fallen nature separated from God. In this fallen state our hearts are separated from God and continually evil. Those who do not respond in faith to God's gracious free gift through Christ live in a fallen state and will be separated from God for eternity. Those who come to Christ in faith are made new creatures and will live in heaven for all eternity. All people sin and are in need of God's continual grace and forgiveness. Sin is an ongoing problem that must be dealt with in the life of the believer through the cross of Christ and not of works. Jesus took on our sin that we might become His righteousness. God is actively at work through the Holy Spirit in the life of the believer, renewing his mind and maturing his spirit, "till we all come to the unity of the faith and of the knowledge of the Son of God, to a perfect man, to the measure of the stature of the fullness of Christ" (Eph. 4:13, *NKJV*).

• God is a sovereign God who is able to do "exceeding abundantly above all that we ask or think, according to the power that worketh in us" (Eph. 3:20, *KJV*). The reason we may not experience this reality is not due to a lack of power but rather to our not appropriating the power that is available. When we seek to do ministry in our own power, nothing divine happens.

IMPORTANT NOTICE

This book is an introduction to Theophostic Prayer Ministry. Reading this book WILL NOT equip you to do this ministry. The purpose of this book is to introduce you to the concepts and principles of this ministry but not provide the "how to" of administering the process itself. Please do not attempt to do this form of ministry based upon what you read in these pages. If you desire to be trained in Theophostic Prayer Ministry you can obtain the Basic training seminar by calling 270-465-3757 or by visiting the web site at www.theophostic.com.

Introduction

Shari had come to talk with her pastor about the
depression and anxiety that she had been experiencing
over the last few months. She was already taking
medication for her panic attacks, and it had helped some,
yet subtle fears dogged her daily. Shari had tried to pray
more, to read her Bible and to be faithful in attending the
ladies' group at her church each week, yet she was still
struggling. She still entertained occasional thoughts of
suicide and was in deep emotional pain.

Shari did not know it, but her pastor had just
completed a video-training seminar about a new ministry
approach called Theophostic Prayer Ministry. The pastor
was a little uncertain as to whether he should attempt to
use this approach with Shari, as he had not used it before,
but he decided to at least introduce her to the approach.
He began by explaining the basic principles of the
ministry. After listening to the pastor, Shari agreed to
allow him to administer the process.

The pastor prayed, asking for guidance and
discernment, and then used the principles he had learned
to help her follow her fear to its origin in her memory.
Within a few minutes an enormous amount of pain
began to surface and she began to describe a very
disturbing memory of childhood pain and emotional
wounding. At times during the process the pastor did not

7

know quite what to do and felt a little fearful himself. During these moments he would pray and review the principles in the training manual supplied at the seminar he had attended.

After a while he began to see that even though Shari was manifesting intense pain (almost as if she were actually experiencing the event she was describing), she did not seem to be out of control. He prayed softly as she walked through the entire memory, feeling all of its fear and pain. After a time he asked her to describe what she was feeling. She reported immense fear and panic (much like the same panic that had been surfacing in her present life). He asked her to identify what it was in the memory that she believed was causing her to feel what she was feeling. She reported that she believed she was going to die. While tempted to reassure her that she was only in a memory and was completely safe, the pastor refrained. He had learned in the seminar that this would not alleviate her fear and would only cause her to suppress it again, so he remained silent and waited. Instead, he had her embrace the fears and encouraged her to feel them completely.

Little by little Shari came to understand and identify the true source of her pain, which she discovered was not the memory itself but the false beliefs in the memory. She said things like: "I am going to die," "I can't breathe! I'm suffocating," and "This was all my fault." In the midst of her immense emotional and physical pain, the pastor invited the Holy Spirit to reveal truth to her in the midst of her fear and panic. Suddenly everything changed. The pastor watched as a calming wave of peace washed over her. Shari immediately stopped expressing pain; her breathing relaxed, and her countenance changed from one of panic and anguish to one of complete peace and calm.

She looked at the pastor with a smile of relief and sighed, "It's finally over. I now know that I am not there anymore. Jesus said I was not bad or shameful. It wasn't my fault. Jesus said that He has removed that pain forever with His truth." She then cried tears of relief and joy, and so did the pastor. He had never seen anyone move from such pain into such genuine peace. He later told the pastor friend who had introduced him to this ministry that, "It was like I was standing on holy ground. It was indeed a very holy moment. God was in that place!"

Shari's story has been and is being replayed thousands of times around the world as pastors, counselors, professionals, and lay ministers are administering a simple yet powerful ministry tool developed in the early 1990s called Theophostic Prayer Ministry.

What Is Theophostic Prayer Ministry?

The term *theophostic* comes from two New Testament Greek words T*heos* (God) and P*hos* (light). These two words describe God illuminating a previously darkened area of one's mind and thoughts with His truth. Theophostic Prayer Ministry is God's true Light, the Spirit of Christ bringing divine truth experientially into one's historical life experiences.

Theophostic Prayer Ministry is not new in concept only in intention. God has been operating on these same principles though out history. He desires His people to walk in truth and know His peace continually. Though out the ages God has allow and often caused his people to encounter difficulties which exposed their false thinking and wayward behavior. In the midst of these trials and exposure His true children were motivated to cry out to Him where He has been found faithful to illuminate their minds with His truth and draw them into His presence and peace. Theophostic Prayer Ministry is a systematic and intentional cooperation with what God is doing in the trials we face that expose us. Theophostic Prayer Ministry is focused and intentional mind renewal at the experiential level.

Some people have confused the name Theophostic with some other groups using the Greek word for God (*theos*) that are not Christian based and are, in fact, New Age. As you will soon discover, this ministry approach is centered on Jesus Christ, His truth, direction and orchestration.

Theophostic Prayer Ministry is a process in which the Holy Spirit reveals specific and personalized truth to the wounded mind of the one seeking freedom. This truth never supercedes, adds to or takes away from what has already been revealed in the written Word, but rather personalizes the same for the uniqueness of the individual and his or her situation. In its simplest description, Theophostic Prayer Ministry is prayer. In the context of prayer the minister moves aside and allows the Spirit of Christ to expose darkness with light. It is Spirit of Christ revealing truth, freeing an individual of the lies that dominate his or her thinking, emotions and behavior. Jesus can set people free from lifelong fears, shame, false guilt, and anxiety, lifting the dark clouds of all emotional pain in a divinely directed moment. This is basically Romans 12:2, "Be transformed [changed] by the renewing of your mind."

Theophostic Prayer Ministry focuses on the origin of our pain, not on the emotional symptoms or the consequential behaviors of our lie-based pain. During the ministry session, ministry facilitators don't give advice, quote Scripture or tell the person in pain the truth, since this rarely has much impact in such context. Instead, the minister allows the Holy Spirit to reveal His specific and personalized truth to the person in pain, because that's what the wounded person needs — a healing word from God. Later, after the session, discipleship and biblical instruction can be offered and be beneficial.

I (Ed Smith) spent many years seeking to help people with emotional pain by giving them my take on the truth. I prayed with them, quoted Scripture to them, counseled them, provided steps of action, made assignments, provided books to read, tapes to listen to, encouraged them and yet they still remained in pain. It wasn't until I admitted my inadequacy and depended on Christ alone to free people that I began to see more consistent miracles occur. This does not nullify the necessity of biblical instruction or all the other things I did but it does suggest that there is a time and place for both.

I personally burned out trying to care for the deeply wounded who were coming to me for help using the above-mentioned approaches. Now I enjoy watching the Lord Himself meet people in their places of pain with His truth and lasting peace. On the other hand I also enjoy providing biblical instruction to those who are walking in genuine freedom and peace in places where all they knew before was emotional duress and defeat.

Please hear me clearly in what I am about to say. *I am not* saying that without Theophostic Prayer Ministry people cannot find freedom, be released of their lies, or walk in true victory. God uses many different forms of

ministry to accomplish His work in His Church;
Theophostic Prayer Ministry is but one of many.
However, I am saying that apart from the Spirit of Christ
accomplishing His experiential work in me, no effort,
work, or discipline on my part will ever accomplish the
renewing and spiritual maturing that God intends.
Christian growth and maturity is not a "you and me,
God" endeavor but my being submitted to a "work of
God in me." Spiritual performance is not spiritual
maturity.

Theophostic Prayer Ministry is simply a
systematized model or avenue by which we can move to
a place where God can accomplish what only He can
accomplish. We must never lose sight of the reality that
"it is God who is at work in you, both to will and to work
for His good pleasure" (Phil. 2:13).

Definition of Theophostic Prayer Ministry

**Theophostic Prayer Ministry is intentional and focused
prayer with the desired outcome of an authentic
encounter with the presence of Christ, resulting in
mind renewal and subsequent transformed life.**

"Intentional focused prayer...

Theophostic Prayer Ministry is in its most basic
form simply intercessory and petitioned prayer. It is

focused and purposeful, in that it has a goal and a specific purpose in mind. The facilitator of the ministry session is asking the Lord to enable the ministry recipient to: 1) embrace, own and take responsibility for her emotional pain, 2) to be willing to let go of all defenses and other hindrances that the Lord exposes and that thwart her moving toward God's purposes in the process, 3) to understand, discover and expose the lie-based causes of her emotional duress, and 4) to be willing to hold up everything exposed by the Lord to Him for His release and mind renewal.

...a desired outcome of an authentic encounter with the presence of Christ...

Never in the history of the Church has there been more effective biblical education available to its members. There is a Christian bookstore in nearly every city. The Bible is available in a host of translations and formats that include electronic computer versions that allow mind-boggling quick search features. However, it seems there is a shortage when it comes to people having genuine experiential encounters with God. Our cognitive understanding of God is unsurpassed but it seems we may be a bit anemic when it comes to experiencing the presence of Christ. Receiving truth through discipleship, teaching, and Biblical instruction plays a vital role in the life of the believer. However, on going authentic encounters with the person of Jesus is just as important. One without the other leaves a void. Theophostic Prayer Ministry is focused on encountering Christ but recognizes the need for both. When the Apostle Paul declared, "to know Him and the power of His resurrection" (Phil. 3) he was not referring to gaining more biblical knowledge. He was crying out for experience. Both cognitive expansion and experience are a necessary part of the mind renewal journey.

...resulting in mind renewal and subsequent transformed life."

When people receive truth from the presence of Christ in places where they have harbored lies, the outcome is immediate and radical change in people's lives as a result of mind renewal. They report peace where there was pain and subsequent transformation of their behavior. One of the signs that true renewal has occurred in a ministry session is the evidence of genuine and effortless behavior transformation. If a person has an authentic encounter with God, there should be a noticeable change. If there is not, then the encounter may be questionable.

There is an obvious connection between sinful behavior and emotional pain. I believe that much sinful and otherwise inappropriate behavior is motivated by the emotional duress that people carry. Often poor behavior is a vain attempt at emotional pain management. Too often changing behavior through much effort becomes the focus of many people. When changing behavior becomes the goal, this focus can put people into a perpetual cycle of self-effort, controlled behavior and ultimate defeat. Romans 12:2, Paul declares that changed behavior/transformation is a natural outcome of mind renewal when he writes, "be transformed by the renewing of your mind." Mind renewal is the expected outcome of a ministry session when Christ's transforming truth is received.

How Theophostic Prayer Ministry Began

Before I developed Theophostic Prayer Ministry, I was surrounded by deeply wounded people needing ministry, while I, myself, was becoming defeated and burned out. I would come home each day wasted, without a drop of energy to give to my family. I was meeting with a group of incest victims and knew that the pain they carried was coming from their beliefs or interpretations of the abuse and not the abuse itself. I knew that their abuse was over and not the cause of their present emotional pain. I had tried every means possible to get them to embrace the truth, but to no avail.

I can remember having them revisit their traumatic memories over and over, but nothing significant happened. I watched them abreact in deep emotional and physical pain as they experienced their memories, only to have the pain remain.[1] During this abreaction I tried to give them the truth, but they could not embrace it. I would have them tell me the truth (It wasn't their fault; they were safe now; they were not dirty, shamed, defiled) and acknowledge it themselves out loud, yet they could not make it their own.

For example, if a woman was seeing herself being brutally raped in her memory, I might ask her, "Where are you right now?" Shaking and trembling, she would tell me the truth, "I am in your office."

I would continue, "Are you being raped?"

She would answer, "No, I am safe now."

I would ask, "Can he hurt you now?"

She would respond, "No, I can stop him now. He cannot ever hurt me again!"

I would ask, "How do you feel, now that you know these truths?"

She would respond, "I feel afraid."

I would ask, "Why?"

She would say, "Because he's hurting me and I'm going to die!"

These irrational, illogical responses perplexed me. This woman knew the truth and could verbalize it, yet her *lie-based* thinking residing in her memory would override it all and she would be overwhelmed by terror.

Week after week, hour after hour, I labored with these women, until I came to the end of my self. I was driving home one evening after a group session, tired and very disappointed about what had occurred in the session (which was nothing but more of the same). I remember feeling myself give up and let go of the battle. I cried out in my spirit to God, "I can't do this anymore!"

It actually felt good to let go of the task of helping these women. I began to make plans for what I would do with the rest of my life. My wife, Sharon, and I had already developed a very successful marriage encounter weekend that we were offering to churches across the country. My initial impulse was to pour myself into this effort and gradually end my counseling relationships.

In this place of having "given up," the Lord was finally able to get through to me. As I studied the Scriptures during my prayer times, I began to understand things that I had not seen before. *I am not saying that I had a divine revelation, because I did not.* I simply began to understand Scripture where I had not before. The main truth that I had overlooked in all my years of ministry was so basic and simple that I am ashamed to admit that I had missed it. I actually gave verbal assent to it, but I didn't live it out with my life. The basic truth that I was missing was simply allowing the Spirit of Christ to be present in my ministry sessions. I always prayed both before and after our sessions. However, I never actually invited the Holy Spirit to participate, and never expected Him to address the person in his or her traumatic pain. Here I was, a Christian counselor and minister, and yet I had forgotten about Jesus. What I had done in my counseling practice was the same thing that I had done in the church ministries I had served in earlier years. I had learned to "work the programs," to grow the church in attendance, to keep people coming and keep those in attendance happy, all the while rarely experiencing the presence of Christ.

When people experience the presence of Christ, there is *always* miraculous change. I am afraid that much of what we call spiritual encounters with God are program-driven events, orchestrated and manipulated to create a pleasurable moment for the recipient. Yet, if what we have experienced has not transformed our lives at some level, then it is questionable as to whether we have had a genuine God experience. The emotional response we have during the event is not a determining factor of the validity of the experience. We can have a warm emotional and nostalgic experience at a James Taylor concert. However, this cannot be said to be a spiritual moment. (Sorry, baby boomers, this does not qualify as a God experience.) Each of us can know God experientially in those places where we have buried and carried pain and woundedness.

Who Needs Mind Renewal?

Most people have not suffered a severe trauma, but everyone has been wounded at some level—all of us have memories that are imbedded with lies. We all need our minds renewed. When we experientially "know" God in these places and receive His truth, we will find His rest, joy, and peace. Paul said, "I pray that the *eyes of your heart* may be enlightened, so that you may *know* what is the hope of His calling, what are the riches of the glory of His inheritance in the saints" (Eph. 1:18, emphasis added). As the "eyes of our heart" are opened we will see who we are in Christ and come to "know" the love of Christ experientially.

This is my prayer for you as you read this book. You can find freedom from the lies you believe and walk in His peace. I am not suggesting that the journey will be easy, without effort or determination but He has promised us His peace. "May the Lord of peace Himself continually grant you peace in every circumstance" (2 Thess. 3:16).

Just ask this fellow in the following story.

He had always been an introvert. He would honestly say that throughout his entire childhood he was friendless and desperately lonely. As a child he was branded by his peers as an outcast and a target for their cruel jokes and scornful rejection. The years of continual mistreatment left him with a "landfill" of lies he believed about himself coupled with immense anger and resentment. Later as an adult he was careful to keep people out of his life for fear of further pain. In his early years of adulthood, others viewed him as being aloof, arrogant and uncaring. The truth was, he was lonely, frightened of relationships all the while in desperate need of human relationship. However, as the years passed he learned to bury his pain and perform in a more socially acceptable manner. But he never knew genuine intimacy even with those in him immediate circle to include his wife. He later became a successful minister serving in many different churches for nearly twenty years mastering the skill of performance-based spirituality.

When he first began to receive Theophostic Prayer ministry he was not even sure if he needed it since he had so carefully and successfully buried his pain beyond his conscious awareness. He viewed his lack of emotion (and especially anger) as "self-control" and spiritual prowess. He had come to the place where he actually believed he was "together" and had successfully put "his past behind him." However, as he continued to seek ministry the deep pain he had buried began to surface and became noticeably evident. His renewing journey was initially slow and laborious but rewarded with continual evidence of genuine transformation. Others around him began to report noticeable change as well. He has now been on this mind renewal path for nine years and can honestly say that he is walking in more genuine freedom and peace than he could ever believe possible. If you do not believe him, just ask "me."

You can, too.

Special note to pastors and counselors:

Please understand that this book is *not* training in how to do Theophostic Prayer Ministry. *Please do not* attempt to administer this process with others without having completed the full Basic Training. Many of the primary principles of administering Theophostic Prayer Ministry are not included in this book, and you may experience negative results if you attempt this process without adequate training. This book does *not* contain all you need to administer the process. *You may cause more harm than good if you seek to lead a person to the places of pain in his or her mind without all the tools you need to deal with what you open up.* Please be wise as you minister to hurting people.

Know that training in Theophostic Prayer Ministry or any other similar approach to ministry does not make you a counselor, therapist or qualify you at any level as such. Minister within the parameters of your qualifications, expertise and experience. Lay ministers should seek to minister under the supervision of your pastor or other Christian mental health professional.

Warning: Some of you reading this book may become uncomfortable with a few of the stories that I share. The content of the stories may very well trigger the pain in your own past. If you become bothered by a story, I would suggest that you skip over it until you can be in a place where you can receive qualified ministry and care.

There are distinctions in Theophostic Terminology.
There are many different terms and phrases I use when describing this ministry process. Some are consistent with others' definitions, while I have redefined some and coined others. The terms "healing," "inner healing," and "healing of memories" have been around for a while now and have different connotations for different people. The term healing, when used in regard to Theophostic Prayer Ministry, describes the outcome of mind renewal. For clarity, I have chosen to deliberately avoid the term healing for the most part and replace this term with mind renewal. I believe that the term mind renewal is more

descriptive of what happens in a Theophostic Prayer Ministry session. Mind renewal occurs as the truth of God replaces the falsehoods people believe. When truth is experientially realized, perfect peace follows. As truth is embraced, what was emotionally painful as a consequence of lie-based thinking becomes peaceful, transformed by the Lord's light and freedom. Once the lies are removed from a painful memory, a true metamorphosis/life transformation should be evident in that memory. In a Theophostic Prayer Ministry context, this result would be described as mind renewal.

Chapter One

The Hurt Is Gone —
ALL Gone!

Margaret's Story

Margaret was clearly in intense emotional pain. As she sat in the chair in front of me in my office, she resisted eye contact by either looking away or holding her head down in a shamed posture. Each time I spoke to her, her answers were short and truncated. When I asked her a question, she would hesitate and then respond as if I had called her back from some distant place in her mind. When she answered, her inner pain would become more acute and apparent, as though my questions were forcing her to connect with a painful reality that she wanted to avoid. Her eyes filled with tears and she held tightly to her frayed and wadded tissue, nervously twisting and folding it over and over.

Margaret reported to me that when she was eight years old, her father had begun to sexually and physically abuse her, and he had continued to do so throughout her childhood. Her adult life had been filled with depression and defeat, failed marriages, joblessness and distrust of others. Her doctor had prescribed heavy doses of medication.

In the past I would have told Margaret that she would need to see me for two to five years of counseling, and even then the best she could hope for was to become more functional and live a more productive life. Even after years and years of counseling, the incest survivors with whom I had worked (prior to Theophostic Prayer Ministry) still had some residual pain in their memories and all had some difficulty being sexually intimate with their spouses. Sexual intimacy was a guaranteed trigger that would incite their emotional pain from the sexual abuse.

Today it would be different. Today she would choose to face the lies stored in her abuse memories and embrace the painful emotion thereof. It would be in this painful context that she would also find genuine and transforming peace as she encountered the presence of Christ. She would discover that the "Lord of peace Himself [does desire to] grant [her] peace in every circumstance" (2 Thess. 3:16). She would not be coming back for endless weekly sessions or joining a survivor's recovery group; today she would find freedom from the pain in the abuse memories she surfaced.

I began by asking her if she truly wanted to be free of her pain, and she told me yes. I then shared the Theophostic Prayer Ministry principles and asked her if she wanted to undergo Theophostic Prayer Ministry, and she said yes. I asked her to focus on the emotional pain she was feeling and to see if this emotional smoke trail back to the memories that might harbor the source of that pain. The goal of our session would be to receive a decisive word from the Holy Spirit, which would, in turn, release her from the pain of the lies that were the true source of her emotional discomfort.

Before we began the session, Margaret's traumatic memories had shamed her, condemned her and made her feel dirty, nasty and somehow responsible. Yet as she processed her painful memories, one by one, her emotional pain disappeared as the Spirit of Jesus revealed His truth to her. At the end of the session, I asked Margaret to bring back to mind all the memories of her father molesting her that she had surfaced during the ministry session, and asked her to tell me what she felt. She exclaimed, "It's gone! All the shame, guilt and pain are gone!"

To this day, Margaret reports complete release from the pain and shame she had felt in her abuse memories with which we dealt with that day. Margaret is on the road to genuine freedom.[1]

Paula's Story

Paula was over 70 years old when she came to me for help shortly after one of her relatives had died. She told me that as she had been standing next to the coffin, she had noticed that all the other family members were expressing genuine grief over the man's death. Many had been crying and were overwhelmed with sadness, but all she had felt was rage and a sense of relief that he was dead. The longer she had remained at the graveside, the more her anger had swelled. Finally she had excused herself and gone home.

This experience had confused Paula, and she had come to me for Theophostic Prayer Ministry. She had tried to understand her feelings, but nothing in her conscious mind explained her anger and rage. She was perplexed.

During the Theophostic session an old, forgotten event emerged. Paula reported to me that when she was only eleven years old, a distant family member had snuck into her room one night and forcefully raped her. The pain had been excruciating, and the fear and confusion overwhelming. After the attack, she had quietly cried in the bathroom while she had washed the blood out of her underclothing. She had decided to keep quiet because she felt no one would believe her, since this person was favored and respected in the family. She had also felt a great sense of dirtiness and believed that she had been defiled by what he had done.

Paula buried the memory, but her rage and shame haunted her throughout her life. Her disruptive anger had filled her relationships with turmoil, and she had suffered from addictions, compulsions and four broken marriages. Her anger had finally made its grand entrance at her abuser's graveside. Yet after several sessions of Theophostic Prayer Ministry, Paula's rage was gone and her mind was at peace concerning the abuse. This one consciously hidden event had robbed her of joy for over 60 years, but it is never too late to find freedom from our pain.

June's Story

June came to me suffering from what she described as an irrational fear. I explained to her that I believe that for the most part, there is no such thing as irrational fear. Fear is the natural response to a perceived danger, threat or harm. When we experience feelings of fear for no apparent reason, this is not irrational; it's simply irrational in the present context. When something triggers a lie-based memory, we feel the *rational* fear, shame and guilt of the original event. In its original context it makes perfect sense but in the present context it seems illogical.

June argued that her fear made no sense, saying that for the last six months it had come each night shortly after she went to bed and everything was quiet. She knew she was safe, and couldn't understand why she felt so afraid. I asked her if she had ever felt this same fear in other situations. She said that she had, but it had been under different circumstances and never at night in her bed.

We tried to find the source of her fear but did not get very far in her first Theophostic Prayer Ministry session. However, we were able to reach several memories that held negative emotions, and freedom came to those places. Yet June's fear remained. I asked her to go home and at bedtime to be aware of what her mind focused upon just before the fear surfaced. The next week she reported what she thought was a strange discovery — the fear was somehow connected to her clock ticking by her bed. She also realized that her bedtime fears had begun after she had purchased this clock. Her solution was to get rid of the clock and thereby be rid of the fears.

I realized that the clock was not the problem, and that the ticking had triggered the lie-based pain of a painful memory. I asked her to think about lying in her bed, listening to the ticking of the clock and to allow the fear to surface. Within a few moments she felt the fear. I applied the Theophostic principles, and within a few moments she found herself in a frightening memory from her childhood she had long tried to forget. As a little girl, someone had come into her room, molested her and threatened to kill her if she screamed or made any noise. While the trauma was happening she had endured the event (dissociated) by focusing on the ticking of a grandfather clock that was in her room.

Her newly purchased clock had become a nightly trigger that surfaced the fear and pain contained in the memory of that childhood experience. As June was willing to go through the memory, feel the fear and identify what she had believed about the abuse (false interpretation), we invited the Holy Spirit to reveal His truth to her. As she received His truth, the fear vanished and His perfect peace took its place. Later she reported that the clock no longer triggered any fear, and she was having peaceful and restful sleep. She had also decided to keep the clock as a reminder of God's renewal and healing.

Sandra's Story

Sandra had been in and out of mental hospitals and was heavily medicated. Overall, she was an emotional wreck. She could not work and lived with her parents even though she was 30 years old. Her misinformed yet well-meaning pastor had warned her to stay away from Theophostic Prayer Ministry. He had read some of the misinformation and criticism circulating on the Internet. Nevertheless, out of curiosity, she had looked up the word *theophostic* on the Internet and had found our Web site: www.theophostic.com. (It is incredible how God takes that which is designed to discredit this ministry and uses it to bring about good.) What she read on the Web page was contrary to what her pastor had told her. As she read the testimonies of others who had reported restoration from their lifelong emotional struggles, she felt hopeful for her own situation.

When Sandra came to my office she was as emotionally downtrodden as any person I had ever seen. She handed me a stack of medical records that documented her journey over the last fifteen years. She had already spent thousands of dollars out of her own pocket over the many years of treatment, yet she was still in great distress. Her extensive medical and mental health records, from a host of counselors and doctors, revealed a list of diagnoses that included chronic depression, obsessive-compulsive disorder, panic disorder and several phobias. She sat quietly and non-responsively as I skimmed through her file.

When I finished I laid it on the table beside me and asked her to look up at me. Her eyes were empty and filled with despair. I looked into her eyes and asked her what I ask everyone who comes to see me, "Sandra, do you want to be free of your pain? Do you want Jesus to release you?" I needed to know what her will was in the moment. Not everyone that comes for help wants to be free. She slowly but clearly responded, "Yes." I recognize the absolute requirement of engaging a person's true will when doing ministry. In the Theophostic Prayer Ministry Basic Seminar Manual one of the chapters is titled "The Human Will; the Second Most Powerful Force in the Universe." Though God is of course the most powerful force there is, He has limited His omnipotence to our choosing. Something or nothing always happens in a ministry session because of the person choosing. I went on to say to her, "If this is true that you desire freedom, then you meet all biblical requirements — faith and willful submission to Him — as far as I can tell, for God to release you of your pain." I went on to ask her, "Are you willing to go to any memories that hold the source of your pain? Are you willing to feel all of the pain and identify the true reason for why you feel the way you do?" There was a longer pause before she responded, but eventually she spoke with a clear and firm "yes."

Sandra had scheduled several sessions with me, which is what I recommend for those who are highly traumatized and have a lot of trauma memories. (Keeping in mind that mind renewal is a life-long journey that includes both cognitive learning and experiential encounters with Christ as is reported in but not limited to TPM sessions.) Day by day, we visited memory after memory, for hours on end, walking through some of the most horrific experiences that can be imagined. The presence of Christ came into each and every memory, in the midst of seemingly endless pain, bringing perfect peace with His truth. At the end of the three days, Sandra said that she felt peace and genuine release.

Sandra's initial visit with me was over four years ago. She is no longer depressed, she is no longer dissociated and she is no longer obsessive. I still see Sandra from time to time, because we live in the same town. When she experiences pain because of additional lie-based memories, she comes to see me in order to bring Christ's renewing to those memories as well. Mind renewal is a lifelong journey as God continually exposes our lie-based thinking so He might release us with His truth.

Some might suggest that when I ask a person to look for the source of their present pain that I may be implanting a false notion that a painful memory is present when in fact there may be none. I trust the neurological principle of association to be true and valid in this context. I believe that everything we know, feel, think or perceive is connected to life experience and thus my present state is in some form associated with my past.

We have no mental information that did not come to us originally by way of experience. Thus what a person feels in the present moment is connected to something that he or she has already experienced someplace, sometime. The present feeling is connected to a belief that he or she arrived at somewhere. Even if a person believes that what he or she feels is limited to the present situation, this present moment is actually history in that it has already occurred and thus it too is memory. If we are going to help people in emotional pain with any counseling or ministry approach we have no other option but deal with memory since everything except the actual present moment is past tense and only accessible as memory. Some people suggest we just put our past behind us. If we actually could do this we would have nothing from which to live in the present. Every thought in our minds is rooted in our past. All we have are memories and the immeasurable moment we call the present tense.

Margaret's, Paula's, June's and Sandra's stories are typical of those who receive Theophostic Prayer Ministry. The renewal experienced is genuine and lasting. I receive literally thousands of emails, cards and letters from people all around the world who are using this approach to ministry and are giving witness of the glorious things that God is doing in the lives of wounded people.

Note: Though all the above stories where about sexual abuse, the efficacy of Theophostic Prayer Ministry is not limited to this type of emotional wounding. Theophostic Prayer Ministry is applicable to any area where lie-based thinking is at the root.

One Episode of My Story

A few years ago, I was at a conference listening to a speaker making a presentation. Some of the things he was saying caused me to emotionally react in a negative way. As I sat there listening, I noticed a growing anxiety and a tightness in my chest. In the past I would have dismissed this and suppressed my feelings, often covering them over with anger or feelings of offense. I have learned that many negative emotions, such as fear, helplessness, anxiety and worry are often hidden by anger. I got up from my seat and went into a small back room. As I sat in the chair, I allowed myself to feel the increasing anxiety. I began to apply the principles of Theophostic Prayer Ministry and soon discovered the memory in which I had first felt that same emotion.

I remembered a time from the second or third grade when I was on the playground. Two children had been appointed to choose sides for the game we were about to play. I was the very last child to be chosen for a team. I watched as the team captains argued over who had to have me on their team. I felt rejected, unloved, not good enough and angry. The messages underneath these feelings were lies that I believed, and were the source of the pain I was experiencing. I continued with the Theophostic process, and soon the Spirit of Christ revealed these words to my heart and mind: *I love and want you and I chose you.* The instant I understood these words, the anxiety and tightness in my chest vanished. I went back into the conference and listened to the rest of the lecture without any further noticeable emotional reaction.

My memory of what happened on the playground is not traumatic, was not about abuse and yet it contained lies that were hindering my adult life. I share this personal experience to say that mind renewal is for everyone, not just those who have been traumatized with abuse. I am just like you; when I feel bad feelings, I am prone to make poor decisions and act out my pain. However, the more I find freedom and am released to walk in God's perfect peace, the better equipped I am to make good choices.

Every person on the face of this Earth is carrying some level of emotional pain. We have all been infested with lie-based thinking. If you think you have not been infected, just ask those who know you. If you become aware of how you are feeling throughout the day, you will begin to pick up on when your lies are being triggered. For example, when that fellow gets your parking place at the shopping center, be aware of what you are feeling. The emotion you feel is likely based in a memory of another time when you felt similar emotion. Maybe you are like me, I did not even know I was in need of ministry. I had buried my pain so deep that I rarely experienced it. Should the pain sneak past my defenses, I would quickly deflect it by blaming others, making rational excuses or quickly suppressing it. Most of us have opportunities for renewal every day (in other words we are exposed in some manner or the other), if we will just watch, feel and listen. I know I do.

If you are hurting or know others who are, Theophostic Prayer Ministry may be the very thing for which you have been searching. Life doesn't have to be a constant emotional struggle. You don't have to settle for tolerable recovery or wait years for renewal of your lie-based pain. You can begin an intentional renewal journey now. As you read this book, I hope that you will be sensitive to areas of your life in which you need renewal. God desires this for you. He desires that you walk in truth and come to know Him experientially.

The Basic Principles of Theophostic Prayer Ministry

This is a very abbreviated discussion of some of the basic principles of Theophostic Prayer Ministry. For a complete understanding of this ministry approach you may choose to order the complete training program. (See ordering information at the end of this book or visit www.theophostic.com.)

Principle One: *Our present situation is rarely the true cause of our ongoing emotional pain.*

More often than not, the emotional pain we feel in the present tense has been triggered by *lie-based thinking,* which is rooted in memory. Lie-based thinking is the false belief one holds in memory learned during a specific life event. For example, a man raised by an alcoholic parent might believe the lie that he was somehow the cause for the chaos in his home and responsible to resolve it. This might in turn play out by him being stressed, anxious and over-reactive to life situations where there was perceived lack of order. If we blame the present situation for the emotional pain coming from the earlier memory event, we will be trapped in an irresolvable cycle of emotional pain and defeat. To believe that other people or circumstances are the cause of our emotional upheaval is to empower them to control us emotionally until *they* change. When we find freedom from the lie-based thinking we will no longer be triggered by it and can walk in peace, content in whatever circumstance we find ourselves (Phil. 4:11).

This is a common scenario in marital conflict. Each partner in the relationship assumes that the pain he or she feels is being caused by the other. When in reality, each one is merely triggering the other's lie-based pain. It is difficult to admit that one's mate is not the source of the pain and that they are only exposing what was already there. It is easier to make someone else the cause than it is to choose to hold myself responsible for the emotional pain in my life. This is not to say that what the other person may have done was inappropriate or justified, for it may not be. However, our emotional response often goes much deeper than the current moment. If what I am feeling is rooted in my own lie-based thinking and I blame another, then I am doomed to suffer in this pain until the other person changes.

Principle Two: *Everything we presently know, feel or are mentally aware of has its roots in a first-time experience.*

This concept does not require a degree in rocket science to figure out. Everything in my brain got there at some point in time. Therefore, anything that I access in the present tense from my thinking had a point of entry. When we react negatively to a present situation, our mind is automatically transferring the negative feelings stored in the memory of the original experience to the present moment that is similar to the original experience. This is a natural neurological process of association that is active during all thinking moments. Our minds are continually networking and linking our present moment to the information learned in earlier places. Our minds provide input as to how to respond to a current situation based upon how we have responded to similar situations in the past. Actually, we respond to the present based upon what we have come to believe to be true within the past events. This automatic superimposing of past emotional responses onto later similar situations will have great bearing on what behaviors we choose to act out. We tend to act out the way we feel. If we act out our present pain, we will likely manifest sinful behavior. This is not to say that some people will deny the pain and choose to act rightly as opposed to acting out their pain. It is merely suggested that many people, much of the time, tend to act out of the pain that has surfaced. For those who choose rightly, they just feel bad while doing the right thing. Both places feel pretty miserable.

Principle Three: *If we try to resolve our present conflicts without resolving our historical lie-based woundedness, we will find only temporary relief for our emotional pain. However, if we find renewal for our past, we can redeem our present.*

Some of today's counseling and ministry methods typically try to change the present behavior of a person by providing new insight and steps of action to modify the behavior they are to carry out. This is often only a stopgap measure and may not result in true and lasting victory if the underlying lies are not addressed. This is not to say that discipleship and teaching are not important, for they are. However, some have been led to believe that controlled behavior is equated with spiritual maturity when in fact many nonbelievers are doing a good job of performing in this same arena. True victory is a work of Christ in us. "I have been crucified with Christ; and it is no longer I who live, but Christ lives in me; and the *life* which I now live in the flesh I live by faith in the Son of God, who loved me and gave Himself up for me" (Gal. 2:20).

It is not based on my effort, determination or willpower but is a natural overflow of His work in me. This does not negate obedience, repentance, discipline or effort on the part of the believer, but rather puts all of these practices in a divine perspective. Salvation is by faith and grace, and so is the walking it out. The apostle

Paul declared that we should walk in Christ in the same manner that we have received Him (see Col. 2:6). Self-control that is provided and maintained as a byproduct or fruit of the Holy Spirit (see Gal. 5:23) is different from controlled behavior that is a fruit of man's effort. When I know the truth and reside in the peace that Christ gives, my "self" is under control as a work of God in me. When I am walking in falsehood and experiencing emotional duress, I have to control myself to keep from acting out on the painful urges. Controlled behavior is better than sinful choices but self control provided by the Holy Spirit is best.

Principle Four: *Since many of the negative emotions we currently feel are reflections of the past, they provide opportunities for the wounds of our lives to be exposed and thus for renewal to occur.*

It is difficult to address that which has not been identified. God will either allow or orchestrate our surroundings to bring us under duress and testing in order to expose what is our true core belief system (see 1 Pet. 4:12-13). It requires little effort to perform at a high level of "spirituality" when things are going well with us. However, when the fire comes, our impurities are made evident and whatever is on the inside (our true belief system) is made evident. These impurities, falsehoods that we believe, will express themselves through our emotional state and consequential behavior. What we truly believe is made evident through our feelings. As I have already stated, we will feel what we believe. If we choose to follow the "smoke trail" of our stirred-up emotions back to their original memory source, we may discover the lie-based belief causing the emotional pain. It is here we can find complete freedom from the emotional pain produced by these lies as we receive truth from the Spirit of Christ.

Principle Five: *To facilitate emotional renewal, we need to identify the three basic elements in the renewal process: (1) the present emotional pain, (2) the original memory container and (3) the original lie(s) implanted in the memory container.*

The present emotional pain is the feeling that surfaces in our current situation when a memory-based lie is triggered. The original memory container is the original event in which the lie-based pain was implanted and stored. The original lie is the belief that was implanted in the original painful memory causing the present pain. Each of these three elements play a part in our thinking, feeling and behavioral responses to life. The present emotional pain is an indicator that a lie-based belief is being exposed. All lies have their original root in a memory source. When the lies contained in these memory sources are identified and exposed to the light of Christ, freedom can follow.

Principle Six: *People are in emotional bondage due to two basic factors, belief and choice. These two factors are rooted in the context of deception.*

This is a very important concept. Belief and choice is the foundation of everything about me. Because I believe the things I do, I make choices. These choices maintain the perpetual cycle of bondage in which I suffer. However, freedom also involves these two primary factors. As I come to know God's truth (belief), I am able to make different choices. Freedom occurs as I receive the truth from the Lord and then choose to walk in it. The one additional element in this truth process is the presence and power of the Holy Spirit. For it is God who grants us new thoughts, leading to the knowledge of His truth which allows us to come to our senses and escape the snare of the devil (2 Tim. 2:25-26).

Principle Seven: *When we believe a lie, the outcome will often have much the same consequences as though it were true.*

The power of a lie is such that if we believe it to be the truth, it will play itself out in our lives as though it were true. Our belief dictates much of our present reality. Therefore, as my thinking changes so does my reality. When the Spirit of Christ brings truth into my thinking, He replaces the lie with truth and I find genuine release and peace where I once only knew pain.

It is common for a person to contain opposing beliefs at the same time. I can believe that I am forgiven for a sin in my life (logical truth) and still feel shameful when I think about what I have done (experiential knowledge). The belief producing the shame has the real power in my life and is also that which will produce the most consequence. My emotional state will point you to my true belief system. It does not matter that what I believe is false; it will have much the same outcomes as though it were true.

Principle Eight: *To be free of the lies we believe, we must identify and own the lies rather than suppress or deny we believe them before we can be free from them.*

Our natural inclination is to deny that we believe lies and to bury the apparent pain they are producing. If we do this, however, we will maintain a cycle of perpetual defeat in our life. As long as lies remain embedded in our minds, they will continue to surface as pain every time they are triggered by situations similar to their original implantation. If I believe that I am worthless and this lie causes me to feel such, I may choose to deny this belief and perform with "confidence" and become an overachiever with notable success (this was my personal experience). On the outside this appears to be a good thing but the purpose of the behavior is to deny and bury what I really hold to be true thus keeping me in bondage. Freedom requires that I acknowledge and take responsibility for what I believe and feel its corresponding emotional pain. I must choose to lay down my feeble defenses and attempts to deny my pain, project the pain onto others or onto life circumstances. In this honest context, God is released (by my will) to free me.

Principle Nine: *In the midst of our "darkness," we must come to realize how utterly bound we are to the lie and how helpless we are to overcome its debilitating grip on our lives apart from God's divine intervention.*

As we experience the emotional pain in the memories, we realize that we are helpless, we are trapped in our emotional bondage and we cannot make the pain go away. This is the same place people in the New Testament were when Jesus healed them physically. It is the same place Paul found himself when Jesus spoke truth into his painful circumstance when He said, "My grace is sufficient for you, for power is perfected in weakness. Most gladly, therefore, I will rather boast about my weaknesses, that the power of Christ may dwell in me" (2 Cor. 12:9). When we try to break free through self-effort and working hard, we will eventually fail. We have no more ability in ourselves to overcome the sin and lies in our life today than we did before the cross. Christ in us is our power to overcome, not self-effort. Freedom is not a "you and me, God" process, but an "I am weak, but He is strong" realization.

Principle Ten: *No person, including ourselves, is capable of talking us out of the lies we believe. We will be free only when we receive the truth from the One who is Truth (John 16:12).*

God is not limited in the ways he chooses to deliver His truth to us. Theophostic Prayer Ministry is but one method He uses. However, much of the training seminars and self-help books being written are based on the idea that if a person can be helped to see what is wrong in his thinking and be provided with truth, he can then choose to replace his false thinking with the truth and change his life. Cognitively receiving truth may have little or no impact on releasing a person from the lie-based emotional pain in his life unless it is delivered to the heart by the Holy Spirit. It is incorrect to assume that people can walk in victory by making right choices and trying hard. Self-effort and controlled behavior can achieve moment-to-moment abstinence but not true victory. Such thinking lies at the heart of works-sanctification and is the basis for most other world religions. The truth is, most people already logically know why they are in pain and logically hold the truth they need, yet they are still in emotional misery and still cannot find their way to freedom.

When I was preaching regularly from the pulpit, I never ceased to be amazed how I could deliver what I thought was a life changing message and then no one changed. However, on one of my bad days where the sermon fell flat, people might respond and experience true transformation. My conclusion to this was that when the Holy Spirit is speaking to people who are listening, glorious things always happen. My best sermons may not move people, but when the Lord speaks, hearts are revived. Theophostic Prayer Ministry simply encourages people to listen as the Lord reveals His truth to their hearts and minds.

I believe 2 Timothy 2:24-26 is one of the clearest passages in the Bible that describes this process. Here the apostle Paul gives instruction on helping someone who is believing falsehood. "A servant of the Lord must not quarrel but be gentle to all, able to teach, patient, in humility correcting those who are in opposition, [if God perhaps will grant them repentance. The original meaning of repentance being a change of thinking], so that they may know the truth, and that they may come to their senses and escape the snare of the devil, having been taken captive by him to do his will."

Notice that we as ministers or "servants of the Lord" are called to teach and correct those who are in opposition (this is discipleship), but it is God who accomplishes the task of setting them free. For until "God grants them *repentance* [change of thinking]" they cannot come to "*know* the truth." It is important to note that the word translated "repentance" here is not necessarily "turning from sin" as is often understood but rather the changing of one's thinking. The *Dictionary of Biblical Languages, Theological dictionary of the New Testament* and the *Enhanced Strong's Lexicon* all define repentance as "change of mind which results in change of life (style)."[2] The word "know" here means to embrace experientially as oppose to having just logical mental assent. This is the same word that Mary the mother of Jesus used when she said to the angel that she had not "known" or had intercourse with any man.

We ministers have an important role in leading people to the place where they are willing to submit themselves unto God and receive from Him. However, unless He grants them repentance or a change of thinking, they will never be free. When God grants new thought, people come to "know the truth" and "come to their senses" and thereby "escape the snare of the devil" (the snare is the lie-based thinking). The words translated "coming to their senses" can also be understood to mean to "sober up" or see clearly. Those of you who have already administered the Theophostic Prayer Ministry process know exactly what this looks like. You have probably already watched people in deep pain crying out in their painful memory suddenly "sober up" and enter into complete peace and clarity of mind as the Lord reveals to them His truth. As the Lord grants "change of thinking" the raging swell of pain becomes a placid calm. This verse contains the essence of what is taught in Theophostic Prayer Ministry.

Principle Eleven: *When we know the truth experientially, having received truth from God in our memory experience, we can walk in genuine maintenance-free victory in these areas of our lives.*

The areas of our minds that are renewed with truth will no longer be stirred up with lie-based pain. Since our emotional pain is a primary motivator for our inappropriate behavior, we are able to walk in permanent and maintenance-free victory in these specific places when our lies and painful emotions are no longer present. Knowing the truth experientially frees me to walk in my present righteousness so that I might experientially agree with the apostle Paul who declared, "Do not let sin reign in your mortal body so that you obey its lusts, and do not go on presenting the members of your body to sin as instruments of unrighteousness; [which I tend to do when I am emotionally stirred and in pain] but present yourselves to God as those alive from the dead, and your members as instruments of righteousness to God [which is effortless when I am walking in the truth and peace of the Spirit]" (Rom. 6:12-13). When I say maintenance-free victory I am referring to the fruits of the Holy Spirit that are produced not through my self-effort, but as a natural byproduct of the abiding truth of Christ and His residing peace.

Principle Twelve: *In times of crisis or in emotionally charged life situations, our experiential knowledge tends to override our logical truth.*[3]

Experiential knowledge (not necessarily truth) is that which I have come to believe through experience. This knowledge is primarily my interpretation of the experience more so than the details of the event. For example, if I was abused as a child my experiential knowledge may be that I believe that I am dirty and shameful. Logical truth is that which is confirmed truth learned through cognitive processes such as personal study and biblical instruction. The power the *experiential knowledge* holds over the *logical truth* is in the painful emotion, which is often attached to the knowledge learned in experience. I can know logically that God loves me and has forgiven me of my sins and yet not be able to shake the bad feelings of worthlessness, rejection, self hate or shame attached to the lie-based thinking in my experiential knowledge held in memory. When these lies are triggered, I have no choice but to feel their pain. Some suggest that we should just deny these feelings and walk in victory. Although some practices this, most would confess that this approach is lacking joy and fulfillment.

It is difficult to appropriate logical biblical truth if what we have learned experientially is contrary to our logically held truth. But as we go to the lie-based sources, discern the lie and receive the experiential truth God has for us, we can readily appropriate the logical truth of Scripture we comprehended only cognitively before. It is easy to logically believe that we are loved and fully accepted by God when we experientially hear Him tell us "I love you" in our painful memory experiences. This is not to say that we should not choose to obey the truth and do what is right even while in the midst of our emotional pain. However, while obedience in the midst of lie-based pain has merit and is praiseworthy, it is better to be able to obey from the heart without having lie-based pain in our face. This is effortless victory that comes when the knowledge of our experience lines up with what we already know logically.

Principle Thirteen: *Lie-based pain can only be removed as the lies causing the pain are replaced with truth, whereas, sin-based pain can only be dealt with through the cross of Jesus.*

The only cure for sin is the cross. This pain is different from the pain one carries as a consequence of lie-based thinking. Theophostic Prayer Ministry does not minimize the role sin plays in the life of a person. If we sin, we will and should feel pain. However, it is not an either or but a both situation. The writer of Hebrews said that we must "Lay aside every encumbrance [weighty things and lie-based pain] and [both] the sin which so easily entangles us, and let us run with endurance the race that is set before us" (12:1).

Principle Fourteen: *Mind renewal is a lifelong process.*

People *cannot* be released of all their lie-based pain in a single session of Theophostic Prayer Ministry. Some have suggested that I teach that they can, but this is not true. In reality, total release would not even be possible within a lifetime. All of us have an abundance of lies that are harbored in our minds. It could require a lifetime to address all that the Lord would eventually expose in us, that is, if we choose to cooperate with Him. I have often said that the finish line in the renewal process is at one of two places; either when we die or when the Lord returns. However, it is very possible for people to find complete and lasting victory and residing peace in *specific* areas of their emotional pain as their lies are replaced with the Lord's truth. It is also common for people to experience increased levels of emotional duress as they allow the Lord to expose the pain that they have kept hidden and suppressed. It is because of this that some have suggested that Theophostic Prayer Ministry causes people to worsen in their emotional state. The truth is that some people may become more emotionally stressed as they are willing to feel what they have denied for so long. As people become willing for the Lord to expose their inner thoughts, they are often surprised to discover just how much pain they have carried throughout their lives. Personally, I have been amazed at the pain that I have carried all my adult life, even though for many years in my Christian life I genuinely thought that I had it all together. Rarely a day goes by that the Lord does not expose some level of my lie-based pain. I am a "landfill" of lies that He is committed to exposing and renewing with His truth. As a result of what the Lord has done, there is no question that I am in a better place today in my spiritual journey than I have ever been before, even though there were times when I thought I was in worse shape than when I started.

I am not suggesting that Theophostic Prayer Ministry is the only way to accomplish this level of renewal in people's lives. Theophostic Prayer Ministry is a systematic way of leading people to the place where God has always been. He resides in truth and rewards those who seek Him. This is nothing new in relation to what God has been doing within His people all along. Theophostic Prayer Ministry is merely an avenue or process for effectively appropriating one aspect of God's process of mind renewal and sanctification.

> **Note:** Though many of the examples in this book are about traumatic abuse, this author does not assume that all people or even most people have suffered trauma in childhood. He does believe that all of us are in need of mind renewal and are infested with lie-based thinking no matter our childhood experience.

Chapter Two

Genuine Recovery Versus Tolerable Recovery

What Is Tolerable Recovery?

I was raised Southern Baptist and served in their churches for over 17 years before beginning a counseling ministry in 1991. After almost five years of working with adult incest victims and seeing only marginal progress and recovery, I was burning out. I believed that the best any person in emotional pain could hope for was to get better, and that renewal from the deep wounds caused by things such as sexual abuse would take years and years. I honestly did not think true resolution from traumatic memory was possible. It seemed more reasonable to teach people how to compensate and live life in spite of one's losses.

My approach to helping people was similar to most traditional Christian counseling practices. I sought to understand why a person was in trouble, conflict or pain, and looked for ways that the Bible could be applied to his or her particular situation and thus give good advice. I saw myself as a troubleshooter of human issues and a biblical applicator to these troubled places. I rightly believed that people were in emotional pain, conflict or trouble because they either had sinned or believed lies, which produced a predictable emotional upheaval from which they would make their choices, resulting in more problems and more emotional pain. I believed that their only way of escape was to know and act on truth.

For many people, getting better is not such a bad place to be. For example, the medicated sufferer of emotional pain is happier being chemically stabilized after years of highs and lows. Emotional stability is a welcome improvement. Feeling better is an improvement. However, I call this *tolerable recovery* and what I offered all my ministry life to those who came to me for help. However, this is not what Jesus offered people.[1] This is not to say that in some cases medication is the right and only choice (apart from a divine intervention), but medication has its limits and not all that have been prescribed provide valid treatment.

More Knowledge Does Not Necessarily Equal More Freedom

Many ministers and counselors are successful in discerning the core beliefs that cause a person pain. The problem is not in discovering the reason for one's pain, but in knowing what to do when it is discovered. Traditional counseling tends to focus on helping people by supplying them with new knowledge, developing new habits and skills, cultivating better methods of communication, overcoming bad habits through support and maintaining some level of abstinence. This has its place in the total scheme of things but is lacking when solely offered.

Those who believe that people can walk in freedom simply by supplying them with biblical truth alone may have misunderstand what the Bible teaches and overestimate the power of self-determination and human willpower. We cannot successfully keep the Law or apply truth through self-effort. Scripture teaches just the opposite. The Bible says, "When the commandment came, sin became alive and I died" (Rom. 7:9). The Law was given to expose us, not to heal us. Yet we often equate knowledge, controlled behavior, willpower and self-effort with spiritual maturity when in fact this is the foundational stone for all other world religions: self-effort.

I know, because that was exactly my approach to counseling. I believed that all I could do was offer truth and then trust that the person had enough willpower and determination to apply that truth. This approach looked much like legalism and works, and produced only more frustration, hopelessness and defeat. Only those people with strong self-discipline, determination and controlled behavior can have any measure of success. As I just said, the Law of God was not given to save us but rather to expose us and condemn us and to become a "tutor" (Gal. 3:24) that would drive us to the mercy and grace of God found in Christ.

Jesus didn't offer people tolerable recovery. When Christ healed people, the renewal was always complete and total as a result of their faith in Him.[2] When the lame man told Jesus that he wanted to be healed, Jesus healed him and told him to walk (see John 5). Jesus did not say, "My friend, put these braces on your legs and take My arm for support, and come hobble along with Me down to the Jerusalem Physical Therapy Center. In no time you will be walking on your own. Now friend, you must understand, you may walk again, but you will probably have a slight limp. You will never be able to run or dance and you may be required to wear these braces for the rest of your life. Be of good cheer, for at least you won't be sitting here on the curb, begging. You will be in better shape than you are now, and that will be tolerable. Come hobble along with Me, for you are healed . . . sort of. *So take up your bed and limp!*" No, the healing that Jesus offered was complete and maintenance-free. This man did not have to work at walking, focus on his steps or fear relapse—he was healed!

True Christian victory has nothing to do with me—it's God's grace and Christ at work in me. True victory is maintenance-free and is easy because it is not based on my self-effort or willpower. Though Jesus called us to take on His yoke that is light and easy (see Matt. 11:29-30), few Christians would describe their Christian walk as easy. Much of what I believed doctrinally and theologically I rarely realized experientially in my Christian journey. I do not believe that this has to be!

More biblical truth and personal application of that truth does not guarantee true freedom, which is effortless. It may give us all the right answers, yet we may continue to suffer. Some of us are good at saying the words, such as "My God shall supply all your needs" (Phil. 4:19), "I can do all things through Christ" (Phil. 4:13, *KJV*), or "We are more than conquerors" (Rom 8:37, *KJV*), and yet struggling to find entry into their reality. Just because we believe these statements logically does not mean that we know them experientially.

Beyond Truth to Experience

Freedom—*genuine recovery*—comes from going beyond knowledge into experience. We must learn the truths of God cognitively and logically (thus the necessity for discipleship and biblical instruction) but at the same time come to know them and Him experientially so we might discover the truth of who we are in Christ, and thereby come to know the love Christ has for us. God wants us to "know the love of Christ which *surpasses knowledge,* that [we] may be filled up to all the fullness of God" (Eph. 3:19, emphasis added). This goes beyond a cognitive understanding.

I am *not* saying that personal Bible study and instruction aren't valuable or important. The Bible clearly states that we should "study to show [ourselves] approved" (2 Tim. 2:15, *KJV*) and we should "let the word of Christ richly dwell within [us], with all wisdom teaching and admonishing one another with psalms and hymns and spiritual songs" (Col. 3:16). However, knowledge without experience is like faith without works—it is dead (see Jas. 2:17). We need to know God experientially as well as cognitively.

Many have difficulty living the Christian life, not because they lack zeal or determination to do better, but because of lies they believe. They may logically know the truth, but their memories are permeated with lies, and their knowledge of God is cognitive rather than experiential. Every lie we believe hinders us from living effortlessly in the finished work of Christ. When we find freedom from a lie, we can walk victoriously and effortlessly in that area of our life. The lies we believe keep us in bondage to the negative emotions and the behavior that follows.

Jerry came to me very angry with his father and ready to dissolve the family business. He said that all his life his father had been overbearing and critical and had made him feel worthless and inadequate. He said that the way he was treated caused him to feel like a helpless little boy. I told him about the principles of Theophostic Prayer Ministry and asked him if he would be willing to look to see where he had first felt these feelings. He agreed.

Jerry had many different memories of times when his father had said or done hurtful things to him, and in each case lies were implanted into Jerry's thinking. I led him through the renewal process, and as a result, Jerry reported perfect peace in all the memories we had visited.

I ran into Jerry a couple of years later and he shared with me this wonderful testimony. He said he was still in business with his father, even though his father had not changed. Then he told me, "He just cannot stir me up anymore! It's like his words have lost all power to penetrate." He went on to say that he now saw his father as a very wounded, angry and unhappy man. He said that he hoped someday his father would be willing to go to the places of pain where he needed to find renewal. When I asked Jerry if he had to work at maintaining this newfound peace when working around his dad, he told me no. He said that it was effortless!

Like Jerry, we are hindered by the lies we believe from living effortlessly in the finished work of Christ. Every time we find freedom from a lie that has hindered us, we are able to stand victoriously in the healed area of our thinking, without any effort on our part to maintain it.

Genuine Recovery Is Maintenance-Free

Over the last six years my wife, Sharon, and I have *not* worked much on our marriage, yet our marriage is stronger today simply because we have been faithful to go to our own lie-based thinking and have allowed the Spirit of Christ to give us truth. One by one, we are bringing the presence of Christ into our individual lie-based memories, and fewer and fewer things cause us pain or trigger negative feelings. I haven't arrived at total freedom in all areas of my life (all you need to do is ask Sharon about this). Yet I'm freer today than ever before. The truth is, our marriage has not been in trouble. We have merely been exposing each other's lie-based pain. As we are willing to own what is exposed, not blame the other, and allow the Lord to replace our false thinking with His truth, we are finding that we relate very well. The only time we are in conflict is when we are "triggered" by our own individual lie-based woundedness.

True victory is the absence of battle and struggle.
True victory cannot be claimed unless the enemy has
been defeated, the dust has settled, the victory flag has
been raised and the war is over. Victory does not require
me to defend the same territory in future battles.
Tolerable recovery, which includes abstinence, stands in
sharp contrast to the blind man who received his sight.
His response was, "one thing I do know that, whereas I
was blind, *now* I see" (John 9:25, emphasis added). He
did not say, "Once I was blind but now I can see a little
better and am seeing more and more as I continue in my
recovery process, and I am really hoping that I don't go
blind again anytime soon."

When Christ heals, God's Spirit replaces the lies
that are causing the pain with His truth, memory-by-
memory, lie-by-lie. When a counselor or minister
provides truth for the wounded person's mind, the lies
very well may still linger. Cognitive truth is not enough
on its own. If this were the case the Scribes and Pharisees
would have been free indeed. Though they had much
knowledge they lacked experience. Truth must go down
into the heart before it results in true freedom, and
freedom comes from experiencing Jesus. We must grow
in the knowledge of Christ but we also need the
experience of Christ.

Merely fighting against sin, controlling behavior, and
diligently making an effort to overcome may not result in

maintenance-free victory, since victory dependent on struggle is continually dependent on waging the fight. I might call this battle-dependent victory "present victory" or "moment-by-moment victory" in that we are not succumbing to the present temptation but we are wrestling with its draw on us. This too is victory but with the necessity for struggle. Let me be quick to say, resisting temptation, choosing to walk in obedience and truth is indeed victory in the moment and a necessity for each of us who desire to live godly lives. Whenever a believer makes the choice to obey rather than sin he is experiencing victory even if it is through some effort or much effort. We are called to "abstain from fleshly lusts which wage war against the soul" and as we do we walk in victory. (1 Pet. 2:11). This obedient victory is well pleasing and will be rewarded by the Lord in eternity. I do not want the person who may have to battle every day of his life to maintain his obedience, and does so, to feel that his success is a second-class victory or not true victory at all. I believe if anything God will reward him all the more for his faithfulness under extreme and lasting pressure. If God will honor him, I would never want to discourage him by suggesting that he is not truly victorious?

However, I would suggest that there is also a victory that is effortless for the believer in the places where the Word of Christ dwells (Col. 3:16), where the Spirit of truth rules, and where the believer can actually rest. This victory can be experienced in specific areas of life where once the vain hope for squelching emotional pain was sinful choice and behavior, driven by emotional pain and aroused by sinful temptation.

It is obvious for each of us that there are areas of sin in which other people struggle that we ourselves never give a second thought to. For example I do not struggle today with the temptation to smoke cigarettes though many people do and I use to. Why is this? I believe that there is a reason that I struggle in some areas but face no temptation in others. There were areas in which I used to struggle but today give no thought. There are some areas in which I have maintenance-free victory without any battle. I believe that at least in many cases, this absence of temptation in particular areas of life is directly linked to resident lie-based thinking and the corresponding pain these lies produce. Where there is emotional pain, temptation to resolve this pain through sinful behavior crouches nearby. It is no coincidence that the Apostle Peter warns us to be alert for the "roaring lion" in the context of suffering (1 Pet. 5). When the fire is turned up whatever we believe will become evident. If we believe lies we will experience emotional duress to match these beliefs. Providing a way to escape this pain is what the roaring lion does best.

This effortless victory is most available in areas where the sinful behavior was the predictable choice of action taken in defense, such as is commonly seen in marital conflicts and other relationships. I know that this is true in my own life and especially in my marriage and in relationship to my father. There are places today that used to be guaranteed "landmines" of relational conflict with both my wife and my father. Whenever certain things were spoken, actions taken or assumptions inferred I had uncontrollable emotional pain surface in my inner being. This emotional pain was a knee-jerk reaction to the lies I believed. This emotional duress created a major conflict in my mind concerning whether I would act out in defense (which I usually chose to do) or grit my teeth and bear it. Sometimes I experienced "present-victory" by not choosing to act out the emotional pain, but it was always a struggle. However, as Sharon and I have chosen to go to our own lie-based emotional pain and have found His truth, many of these places are no longer a problem in our marriage. There is truly "effortless victory" in many places where we only knew struggle and conflict before. Today, the relationship I have with my father appears to be conflict-free and has been for about the last five years, and I do not have to do anything to maintain it. The only reason that I can give for this victory is that I now know experiential truth and residing peace in the "little boy" memories that once carried emotional pain. The good news in my marriage is that we no longer even have to work at these places that were always before guaranteed trouble spots. I have "maintenance-free victory" in these specific places.

I believe that as you seek to allow the Lord to expose the painful places in your thinking you can have this same victory. In the meantime, you must still choose to walk in the truth you know, resist the temptations sent your way, and choose to "walk in a manner worthy of the Lord, to please Him in all respects, bearing fruit in every good work and increasing in the knowledge of God; strengthened with all power, according to His glorious might, for the attaining of all steadfastness and patience; joyously giving thanks to the Father, who has qualified us to share in the inheritance of the saints in Light" (Col. 1:10-12).

Let me say clearly that Theophostic Prayer Ministry will not result in complete recovery of all wounds in a single session. I am also not saying that by going through a few ministry sessions that you will be free of all struggles in your Christian life. I am merely suggesting that you can know real and lasting maintenance-free victory in places in your Christian life. I know this is true because I have and do enjoy this as never before. In later chapters you will read several stories of people who spent many hours and many sessions going through the Theophostic process in order to identify and replace the lies embedded in their memories. Freedom comes memory-by-memory, lie-by-lie. I have been actively and intentionally pursuing my own mind renewal using Theophostic Prayer Ministry for many years. As I am stirred emotionally, I follow the pain to its memory source. I am finding peace in each place I go.

Some people come to me with years of trauma-filled memories piled one on top of another. I may spend many sessions with a person who has experienced numerous traumatic events, but I also see instantaneous recovery *memory by memory* in each session. Even though it may take many sessions with some people, when a person is led to the position where he or she is ready to receive from the Lord, incredible results will occur.

The goal of Theophostic Prayer Ministry is coming to know Christ. As the apostle Paul declared, "I count all things to be loss in view of the surpassing value of knowing Christ Jesus my Lord" (Phil. 3:8). It is uncanny how the truths that people report having received during a ministry session all seem to reflect either the nature or character of God. People are not just receiving truth, they are coming to know Him experientially. I can memorize the passage that God will supply all my needs, but it is another thing to experientially know this reality. My children never have the thought of whether they will be fed each day because they "know" me. They know I will provide.

When Is a Person Completely Free?

Where is the finish line for this process? When does a person become completely whole? Mind renewal is a lifelong journey. The finish line is at one of two places: when we die or when the Lord returns. However, we can go to the places where the lies are stored and find release, lie by lie. With each lie we remove, we are better able to appropriate the deeper truths of who we are in Christ.

I am learning to be aware of my emotional pain in my daily walk. Today, more often than not, I am choosing to allow the Holy Spirit to lead me to the places in my mind where I am harboring lies that are causing me pain. As a result of these choices, I am becoming more and more free! I have come to the place where I have decided that I no longer want people and circumstances to dictate my emotional status. I want to be free and to learn to *be at peace in whatever circumstance I find myself* (see Phil. 4:11). How about you?

Chapter Three

The True Source of Our Emotional Pain

Looking in All the Wrong Places

When we suffer from emotional pain, we usually look in one of two places to determine the source of that pain. We either try to find someone or something in the present to blame or we look to our past and blame those who have hurt us in childhood. However, if we seek to find the cause of our pain in either of these two places, we will never find resolution and never know the peace that God has for us.

If something happens between Sharon and me that stirs up a negative emotion within me, my initial reaction is to blame her and accuse her of being the cause of my pain. I might tell her, "You make me so mad!" or "I wouldn't feel this way if you would just stop this or start that."[1] If it were indeed true that my wife was the cause of my pain, then I could never be free of that pain unless she changed. When we blame another person for our painful feelings, we are giving that person power over our emotions. This doesn't have to be.

Of course, there are times when a person in the present is the original source of our hurt. For instance, if you discover that your spouse has been unfaithful, then much of the pain you feel can be directly attributed to his or her actions. However, similar forms of betrayal that you may have experienced in the past will also surface along with the pain you feel from the present betrayal. If you were abandoned or betrayed as a child, then the pain you experienced at that time will flood the current situation and create an emotional overload.

Emotional overload occurs when a painful situation in the present is inundated with old pain, causing the current situation to feel more painful than it should. When we experience emotional overload, our emotional response will be more intense than the situation may warrant. For example, if a person takes our parking place, our emotional response might call for some mild irritation but not rage. The rage is coming from somewhere else.

Not only do we blame people in our present life for our emotional pain, we also blame the painful childhood experiences themselves. While this might seem logical, especially considering all the horrible things that some people have endured in their childhood, past events are not the present source of our pain. While it's true that had an incest victim been raised in a happy, loving and caring family, he or she would be in a different emotional place today, the actual abuse and mistreatment that person received in childhood is not the present source of his or her emotional pain today.

Granted, the initial abuse did cause a traumatic reaction and may have been physically and emotionally overwhelming, but the event itself is not the *present* source of the person's emotional state. If it were, then abuse victims could never find peace because they could never undo what had been done to them in the past. They would always be victims of abuse, no matter how long they lived or how much ministry or how much counseling they received. The original trauma may have been physically painful, but the body has healed. Original trauma doesn't cause lingering emotional pain. Rather, *the source of our present pain is found in the interpretation we have given the event.* For example, if I feel shame when I think about being raped, it is not the event but rather what I believe about the rape that is producing the shame: *It was my fault.*

If we find ourselves blaming people in our present life or those who have hurt us in childhood, we will be perpetually emotionally wounded. However, Theophostic Prayer Ministry seeks to discover what we believe, and looks to the Spirit of Christ for freeing truth. Freedom results, not from blaming others or by undoing our past (which is impossible), but from identifying the lies attached to our life events and then receiving truth from the presence of Christ.

The Role of Memories and Pain

The memory is the mind's container of historical data and interpretive information. If the memory holds information that is true, it cannot be changed. So, if it's true that little Mary's grandfather raped her and that she was mistreated at school, abandoned by her mother and raised by an occult group in the deserts of Nevada, these facts will remain in her memory. Facts can't be changed, nor are they the cause of present emotional pain.

Little Mary's beliefs about the abuse—not the abuse itself—are the cause of her pain. If she believes that she caused the abuse, then she will feel guilt. If she believes that the rape defiled her, she will feel dirty and shameful. If she believes that her mother abandoned her because there was something wrong with her, then she will feel inadequate, worthless and unlovable. If she believes that she belongs to the occult, she will feel trapped, helpless and powerless. Mary's beliefs about the abuse are the source of her emotional pain.

Whenever something painful happens to a child, the child will interpret that event and store the interpretation in the memory of the event. Even when the child becomes an adult, his or her interpretation of the painful event becomes the source of present pain every time something or someone triggers the memory. For example, Carol was abducted and raped by a man in her neighborhood when she was 14 years old. Now 36 years old and married, she still has panic attacks when her spouse tries to be intimate with her. When her husband goes on a business trip she becomes so fearful that she calls him several times a day.

This happens because God created our minds to work by way of association. Our minds record both the information of the events and our interpretation of the events. That means that many of the experiences we have as children have been stored in our experiential memory bank, along with our emotional responses to the event. Any time someone says or does something, or any time something happens that consciously or subconsciously reminds us of a similar situation in our past, our mind brings this information to the forefront and we feel what we felt the first time it happened.

Memories that are not easily consciously accessible are as powerful and dictating as conscious memories; it doesn't matter that we aren't conscious of them. When something occurs that is remotely similar to the original event—even a word or a look—the original lie and emotions may emerge, causing discomfort. When we experience an event, our brains not only record the expected physical detail of the situation, such as who, what, when and where, but they also record insignificant elements, such as the color of the person's clothing, someone snoring in the next room, the toy bear on the dresser across the room or the ticking clock as seen in June's story in an earlier chapter. Any of this recorded information holds the potential to trigger the emotional pain we felt during the event. Remember too, it is not the details of the memory that carry the emotional pain but rather the interpreted belief. This is why I do not need to see the memory in the present moment to feel its pain. This is why Janice said to me, "I do not know why I do not like my husband to hug me, I just know it makes me feel trapped and panicked when he does."

For example, if during a childhood trauma I fixated on a teddy bear in my room, later when I see a teddy bear in a store it might trigger intense feelings of anxiety. Or if my boss asks me how the report I am working on is coming along, my response will depend on the beliefs I have stored in my experiential data. I may feel inadequate and shamed or feel just the opposite, depending on my history. If I interpreted the original event through lies, then my thinking will be lie-based, and similar events will trigger those same lies.

What Is Lie-Based Thinking?

To understand how Theophostic Prayer Ministry works, you need to understand the concept I have already referred to as *lie-based thinking.* The mind contains information that is a composite of lies and truth. Logically, we know the difference. I know there is no Santa Claus, even though as a child I believed there was. I know that two plus two is four and that Canada is somewhere north of Kentucky. This is what I call logical truth. My logical mind also contains information such as "My God shall supply all your needs" (Phil. 4:19), "The Lord is my strength and my shield" (Ps. 28:7) and "I can do all things through Christ" (Phil. 4:13, *KJV*). I can spout off these verses with ease and impress my Sunday school class with the right answer. Yet while I know these things to be true on a cognitive level, I may not know it on an experiential level. My emotional state in a given situation will expose the difference.

Unfortunately, even though we may know the correct answer in a given situation, many of our choices and responses are based on what we believe experientially and thus feel. If we truly believe that God is our shield and protector, then we should never live in fear. If we believe that God is the supplier of all our needs, then we should never be anxious over finances. If we believe that God is in control of our lives, then we should never worry about what is happening around us.

Yet we can honestly and logically believe all the above and live in fear, worry and uncertainty. What we feel in any given moment reveals the truth about what we truly believe. Our emotions expose our core beliefs.

I do not think it is possible to change our core experiential beliefs through willpower or by simply telling ourselves the truth. Many people have tried memorizing Scripture, posting positive statements on their mirrors and refrigerators, thinking positive thoughts (which are all good things in themselves) and yet still walk around in emotional defeat. We feel what we believe experientially — not logically. As much as we would like to believe otherwise, our emotions will always expose what we truly believe. *If what we believe is false, then it is lie-based thinking.*

The Power of Lie-Based Thinking

What we think dictates how we feel. If we believe a lie is true, then it doesn't matter that it's not, for it will have the same consequences on our lives. If we believe we are shameful because we were sexually violated as children, it does not matter that we were innocent. The shaming lie will work itself out in our lives as though it was true, and the consequences will be the same. Here are some additional examples of this:

One day I was working in our backyard on a project. It was hot and I was tired. My lovely wife came outside to check on me out of kindness and concern. She walked over to where I was working and asked, "Why did you do that like that?" My immediate response was anger — *I do not need her out here criticizing my work!* — and I said, "Why don't you and your criticism go back in the house and leave me alone!" Suddenly the 45-year-old man became a hurting little eight-year-old who was feeling like he could not do anything right.

Years ago, I was serving a church in Kansas City, Missouri, as a minister to single adults. There was a woman who worked as a secretary in the church office who was deathly afraid of spiders. I knew this and teased her from time to time about it. One time I put a big black rubber spider in her top desk drawer as a joke. As it turned out, it wasn't very funny. She found the spider but nearly had heart failure. I felt badly for playing such a cruel trick, but she had no real reason to be afraid. The spider was not a spider at all, yet she believed it was real and because of this she felt real fear and panic . . . of a piece of molded rubber.

Much of this experiential knowing is not always consciously present. What we are thinking at the conscious level is often contrary to what we are thinking and believing at the subconscious, experiential level. When a woman suffering from claustrophobia walks into an elevator and begins to panic, she is not consciously thinking about the time her mother locked her in the closet all day. Instead, she feels the suffocation experienced in the original event as though it were still happening.[2] This forgotten memory contains the source of her panic, but she can give no logical explanation for her present feelings.

Lie-Based Solutions for Pain

Most people are surprised to discover how much their lives are influenced by the lies they believe that were implanted during difficult moments in their childhood. For example, infidelity usually has little to do with the marriage itself. More often than not, the motivation for an affair is rooted in a desire to resolve emotional pain that comes from lie-based thinking.

Before Theophostic Prayer Ministry's inception, I counseled Christian people's infidelity *solely* as a sin problem, as a willful choice of immorality. While adultery is a sin, the feelings driving the decision to commit adultery are usually rooted in a person's lie-based thinking. It and other sinful behaviors are often predictable consequences of deception, producing emotional pain that consummates in sinful choices. James 1:14-15 says, "Each one is tempted when he is carried away and enticed by his own lust. Then when lust has conceived, it gives birth to sin; and when sin is accomplished, it brings forth death." Notice the stages one passes through before a sin is actually committed. First there is temptation or lie-based deception (you are usually tempted only by that which you believe you need or <u>want</u>). Then you are carried away by your own lust. In the original language the word translated here as *lust* does not only suggest sexual feelings, but any strong passion or emotion. When someone triggers my lie-based thinking, my lust or strong emotion is stirred. When I embrace this strong passion, it gives birth to sinful behavior. We tend to make our worst decisions when we are caught up in worry, anxiety, anger, frustration, FEAR, feelings of abandonment, worthlessness, helplessness, powerlessness, etc. We tend to have the greatest difficulty *not* making a decision or taking some action when emotional pain is present. The emotional pain tends to drive us to do something to resolve the duress. This is simply a difficult place to be and where bad things tend to happen. This is why we are commanded to "let the peace of Christ rule in your heart" (Col. 3:15).

This is made obvious in the context of an extramarital affair. While sex is often a consequence of the relationship, it is rarely the driving force behind it. People tend to commit adultery because emotional pain has surfaced in their present relationship and they believe that the adulterous relationship promises some level of relief. When their strong painful emotions are stirred up, they deceptively see the other relationship as a solution to their present emotional pain. Christians and non-Christians alike are often driven by their lie-based pain. Those who engage in affairs experience pleasurable feelings and often mistake them for love. Of course, there can never be love in an adulterous relationship, for how can agape (true love) and immorality coexist? The truth is, most people get married for the same reason they enter into an affair (which is not love). They hope their future spouse will provide them with an ongoing supply of the warm fuzzy pleasure that they have felt while dating and have mistaken for love. This elation is stirred by the hope that the other person will fulfill some perceived need, take away some longing, resolve inner pain, complete that which is believed to be lacking and so on.

Then they get married and fall out of love in a few years (or days) when their partner fails to come through with what they expected and believed their partner should have delivered. As a result, they may be tempted to turn to someone else outside the marriage and repeat the process.

Each partner will trigger the lie-based pain in the other person's mind. When this happens, the partner may look (feel) like someone from the past who has wounded him or her. This is when people start saying things like, "You are just like my mother," "You sound just like my father" and so on.

Just as sex is not usually the motivation for adultery, neither is it usually the motivation for sexual addictions. The sex addict is using sexual gratification as a means for covering a deeper painful emotion. Whenever the painful emotion is triggered, he or she looks to sexual gratification to cover the pain. After a time, this process becomes automatic and appears to be a sexually focused addiction. Yet if you can uncover the lie-based emotion that drives the behavior and follow it back to its source, the person is in a good position to receive the truth, which can break the power of this assumed addiction.

Most addictive disorders have two primary roots. One is the physical addiction of the substance itself. Many people make abstinence the goal, but as I have already suggested, abstinence is not true freedom. It is merely the cessation of an undesirable behavior by way of willpower, determination and group support. People do accomplish abstinence through different programs, and I am in support of this effort, as abstinence is better than sinning, even though it is not true freedom. Yet if the only thing a person does is abstain from his or her addiction, that person is a potential relapse waiting to happen. If a person's lie-based pain ever becomes greater than his or her resolve or if that person loses his or her support system, that person may crumble and there's a good chance that he or she will revert to the addiction or engage in another addiction.

The other primary root of addictive disorders is lie-based pain. Any time that a lie is triggered, it produces the same painful emotion the person felt the first time the event occurred. Somewhere along the way he or she discovered that drinking, smoking, overeating, drugging or viewing pornography masked the pain.

A great amount of what we do when our emotional pain is triggered are efforts in pain management. We may have learned this means of coping from watching others in our family system, or we may have discovered it on our own. No matter how we discovered it, the addiction is not really our problem — in fact, it is our solution for pain.

Abstinence will resolve the physical cravings, for the most part, but it will not remove our emotional pain. If, however, we are willing to look at the source of our pain and discern its reason (the underlying lies), we can find truth. When we know the truth in our innermost parts, the pain will leave and the need to do the addictive behavior will no longer surface.

Paul came to us as a chronic alcoholic. He would stay intoxicated for weeks at a time. This behavior had cost him several jobs and was about to cost him his marriage. His wife had given up on him, was tired and did not want to deal with him any longer. She had already moved out and refused to speak with him unless he got real help.

My schedule was full and I simply could not work him in, so my wife offered to minister with him. Sharon is not a trained counselor and does not profess to be. However, she has completed all the training that is offered through this ministry, and God is using her mightily as a lay minister. She began seeing Paul weekly for about two hours each session. It is important to note that she did not work on his drinking problem. She rarely mentioned it or asked how his abstinence was going. Sharon knew that his drinking was not the problem but rather his nonproductive solution for his emotional pain.

Each week she encouraged him to look back to the deep wounds of his childhood. Paul discovered that as a teenager he had found "peace" for the first time by drinking. As Paul was willing to feel the pain and discern the lies he believed in these earlier memories, the Lord began to give him truth. As each truth entered into his mind experientially, he drank less. After a few months went by he reported that he was not drinking at all.

We saw Paul a couple of years ago. It had been over a year at that time since he had last seen us, and he had not had a drink and reported that it was happening effortlessly. The exciting thing was that he said that he never thinks about it. When there is no pain, there is no need for a solution.

People remain addicted to alcohol or drugs, or maintain eating disorders, because lies remain embedded in their memories. Expel the lies and those suffering from these addictions will be emotionally free. With the passing of time in abstinence, these people may become physically free as well. I do not believe that "once an addict, always an addict." I do not remember the blind man Jesus healed saying, "Even though I can see now, I will always be a blind man." "Once a blind man, always a blind man" is a falsehood. The truth is that this man was once a blind man, but now he can see.

Can you see the problem with making sin or the addiction the focal point in a counseling or ministry session? If I make sin the primary focus and do not address the lie-based thinking, I will be forcing the person to enter into a defeat-confess-repent-adjust-perform cycle.[3] There is a necessity for balance in ministry. Sin can be and often is a problem but so is lie-based thinking. This is not an either/or issue but a grander solution of seeking the Lord's grace and forgiveness for the sins we have chosen to commit and seeking His truth for the lies we believe.

Finding Truth and Freedom

When we follow our present emotional pain back to its *source,* we may find a memory of something occurring that made us feel the same emotion that we are presently feeling. We can find truth and freedom in this place. The Spirit of Christ can reveal His truth to us. Christ removes the lie and replaces the painful emotion with peace. Theophostic Prayer Ministry is a process by which we can discern a person's experiential lie-based thinking and help him or her receive a freeing word directly from the Holy Spirit. When God replaces our lie-based thinking with truth, we can walk in effortless victory, which is maintenance-free. That's what Carla has discovered.

Carla's Story

Carla was an alcoholic attending four AA meetings a week. She was in abstinence but was daily battling the temptation to drink. Her marriage was on the brink and she was flirting with an extramarital relationship. She was on several medications for her mood swings and depression. She also suffered from an eating disorder, and had come to me for help with her present troubles. I asked her if she was willing to look to see where her present pain all began. She said yes. At first we had some difficulty getting to any memories, due to the dissociation in her mind.[4] However, as we processed through the dissociation, a painful reality began to emerge.

Carla reported that her grandfather had molested her when she was between the ages of seven and nine. He would take her on "special" walks and trips. During the abuse, he would tell her that this was the way he expressed his love for her. He was very gentle as he performed oral sex on her. She was confused by this behavior and at the same time did feel a sense of being special. She also experienced feelings of sexual pleasure, causing even more confusion. After it was all over, she felt a deep sense of shame and guilt for what *she had done* with her grandfather.

As a young adult, she often felt deep self-loathing and shame, especially when she would try to be intimate with her husband. She had repressed the sexual abuse but could not suppress the emotional feeling coming from the lies. Her eating disorder had brought her close to death due to malnutrition.[5] She was physically worn out and an emotional wreck.

In our first session we discovered two basic lies in her thinking. One was that she was shameful and disgusting for allowing her grandfather to molest her, since she did not resist or try to stop him. In essence she believed that the abuse was her fault. A second lie was she was a willing participant in the abuse because she felt pleasure during the ordeal and that made her bad.

As a little girl, Carla discovered that if she focused on the pleasure she felt during the oral stimulation, she did not feel so overwhelmed by the shame and guilt of what her grandfather was doing. Yet afterward she felt shame because of the sexual pleasure she experienced.

During a Theophostic Prayer Ministry session, she reported that God had given her this freeing truth: He had created her body to experience pleasure, and her focusing on the physical pleasure was her way of getting through her grandfather's shameful act. She sensed that God told her that she was not dirty or shameful for surviving. This truth replaced her lie-based thinking and Carla's eating disorder subsided, allowing her to progress on through her renewal. Her lies had produced severe pain, which she had sought to manage through destructive behavior. As each lie was replaced with truth, Carla's present life transformed and calmed down, and she was able to walk in true peace and let go of her solution for pain.

Why We Can't "Put Our Past Behind Us"

Many people have tried to put their pasts behind them and not think about them any longer. I tried for 30 years but this approach has never really worked. However, this has not stopped the propagation of this teaching, and as a result some Christians have been misled into believing that they should be able to leave their pasts behind them. Consequently, many of these same people believe that something is wrong with them spiritually because they cannot lay their past wounds at the cross as they have their sins.

This teaching is based upon the statement of the apostle Paul in Philippians 3:13. This is probably one of the most misinterpreted Scripture passages in this regard, and is often used to defend the need to just put our past behind us (and, therefore, negate the need to do things such as Theophostic Prayer Ministry). In it, Paul says, "I do not regard myself as having laid hold of it yet [the resurrection]; but one thing I do: forgetting what lies behind and reaching forward to what lies ahead." To interpret this verse correctly, we must view it in its context.

In this verse the apostle Paul is *not* referring to the wounding or negative experiences that have happened to him over the course of his life. As a matter of fact, he sees great value in the painful experiences of his life and alludes to them often in his writings. When he says he is putting the past behind him, he is not referring to his painful past, but rather the long list of self-attained great accomplishments of his life he has mentioned previously in this same passage. He provides a hefty list of his accomplishments and works in self-righteousness, and says he counts them as rubbish and is putting them all behind him. He says, concerning his life accomplishments:

I myself might have confidence even in the flesh. If anyone else has a mind to put confidence in the flesh, I far more: circumcised the eighth day, of the nation of Israel, of the tribe of Benjamin, a Hebrew of Hebrews; as to the Law, a Pharisee; as to zeal, a persecutor of the church; as to the righteousness which is in the Law, found blameless. But whatever things were gain to me, those things I have counted as loss for the sake of Christ. More than that, I count all things [his accomplishments] to be loss in view of the surpassing value of knowing Christ Jesus my Lord, for whom I have suffered the loss of all things, and count them but rubbish in order that I may gain Christ (Phil. 3:4-8).

If we were to put this into contemporary language, it would read, "I am laying aside every degree, accomplishment, position or status I have obtained in life that elevates myself or leads to self-righteousness and calling it all cattle poop compared to knowing Christ."

Because all of us are emotionally damaged at some level, putting our past behind us is not an option. However, genuine renewal is! Some of us deny and hide our lie-based thinking better than others, but we all need

God's truth to find renewal. It is not a question of whether we are wounded, but rather how extensively we have been damaged.

The cross of Jesus was sufficient for all our sins and emotional wounds, but sins and wounds must be dealt with differently. The trouble is not in the effectiveness of the redemption, but rather in the application of the redemption. God has indeed redeemed us from our sins once and for all, but every day we are in the process of mind renewal as we are being exposed of the lies we believe and being given the opportunity to receive the truth that will release us of our emotional bondages. Until we find freedom from these lie-based wounds, we will struggle with the consequential sins these wounds manifest.

All of us have been hurt by others and through life circumstances at some point misinterpret things that happen. This misinterpretation is the lie-based thinking that cripples us in the years to follow. If my parents tell me that I am not good enough, I will probably internalize this lie. Later, when anyone or anything triggers this thought, I will feel the same emotion as I did with the original wound. This emotional surge will be a primary motivation for the choices I make in each situation. Until the Spirit of Christ reinterprets this experiential lie, I will not be able to live out the reality that I am acceptable, righteous and made complete, since I am raised up with

Him, and seated with Him in the heavenly places in Christ Jesus (see Eph. 2:6).

Choose this day to find the freedom, peace and joy that await you in Christ.

Chapter Four

Theophostic Prayer Ministry: The Renewing of the Mind

A Key Event in My Own Life

When I was in the fifth grade I used to ride home each night on the school bus. We lived about 12 miles out of town. A few days before Christmas break an unfortunate event occurred one evening while I was coming home on the bus. Our bus driver foolishly allowed some of us children to stand up near the door and in the stairwell as the bus was traveling down the highway. That evening as we were traveling down the road, the door suddenly opened. Almost as quickly as it had opened, the driver shut it again and told us all to go to our seats. No one noticed that a little boy who had been standing on the bottom step had been swept out the door and was now lying near death in the ditch by the

95

road. If a passing motorist hadn't discovered his broken body, the boy would have surely died.

The next day at school I was called down to the office, where a series of harsh and uncalled for interrogations took place. To this day I am not certain why I was questioned, but I was yelled at, accused of attempted murder and told that if the boy died (he was still in a coma) my parents would go to jail, along with other preposterous claims and accusations. The experience left me very wounded and filled with lies about my character and myself. I believed that I was guilty even though I wasn't. I believed that when bad things happened around me, people would blame me and think I caused them. I believed that I was somehow bad, though I was not really sure why. These lies impacted my childhood from that point forward. My grades went from As and Bs to all Ds and Fs, all the way up and through high school. These lies followed me throughout my adult life, until the last few years, when I personally received Theophostic Prayer Ministry concerning this memory.

For most of my adult life I did not know that my emotional reaction to certain situations was a triggered response of my mind going back to this particular memory. I did not know that the underlying illogical feelings of guilt I would often feel were coming from this event. I put as much effort as anyone else does into trying to find freedom through prayer, Bible study and diligent determination. However, it has only been since I returned to that traumatic event in my childhood and found God's truth that I have been able to walk in freedom from the fears, anxieties and emotional pain that these lies had created. As I have found genuine renewal of my past in this area of my thinking, my present has been redeemed accordingly and I've found it possible to more fully appropriate the logical truths that I have cognitively accumulated.

Accumulation of Truth Is Not Enough

Our memories contain the information that is stored in our minds. Everything we know, we learned in some life situation, and this presently makes up our reservoir of knowledge. Our memories themselves do not need to be healed, since they are merely the containers of information. Rather, it is the false interpretations contained in our memories that need to be renewed or corrected. The traditional approach to this has been through cognitive assimilation of new data. Many have believed that just receiving cognitive truth could release or change the lies a person believed. This approach has some merit, but for the most part as a stand alone approach, it is simply inadequate. I am not in any way saying that studying the Bible, teaching and instruction are not vitally important, for they are. However, knowledge alone without experiencing the presence of Christ will not result in life transformation. A person can be "bible smart" and yet never know the power thereof. Jesus said it this way when addressing the knowledgeable religious rulers of His day, "You search the Scriptures (knowledge) because you think that in them you have eternal life; it is these that testify about Me; and you are unwilling to come to Me (experiential) so that you may have life" (John 5:39-40 Comments mine). The Apostle Paul said to, "know the love of Christ which surpasses knowledge, that you may be filled up to all the fullness of God" (Eph. 3:19). Knowing the love of Christ is experiential and surpasses knowing about Him. This is not an "either or" issue but a "both and".

As I have mentioned, I have worked with incest survivors for many years. In each counseling session, we would go to their memories, week-by-week, month-by-month and often year-by-year, with little significant change. I told these women the truth over and over, and yet they still carried some measure of residual pain from their abuse. The reason for this, which we will explore more fully later, is that people cannot change experience with data; we can change experience with experience. Theophostic Prayer Ministry leads people to the place where they can experientially encounter the One who is truth: Jesus.

General Thoughts of How the Mind Works

From infancy to adulthood our minds are gathering, assimilating, interpreting and processing the information that they receive. We are either receiving information passively through gathering raw data such as "two plus two equals four," or receiving it experientially, through life experiences, such as being laughed at by our classmates because we wrote "two plus two equals five" on the blackboard by mistake. When information comes to us through experience, our minds couple it with emotion. This emotionally charged information (whether positive or negative) becomes the primary source upon which we rely for future experiential decisions and responses. The non-experiential logical data is passive and void of any real emotional quality, and is used in non-emotional situations, such as doing a mathematical calculation or giving the correct Bible answer in Sunday School.

However, we draw upon the experiential information (and emotion) every time we encounter an experience that triggers the original memory interpretation. Once the original experience is recorded, with its emotional response and belief interpretation, it changes very little over time, even with the accumulation of additional data that is contrary. This original experience becomes the grid from which all similar additional life experiences are measured, interpreted and emotionally experienced.

New experiences tend to confirm what was believed in the original event instead of reinterpreting or augmenting it. If my original experience was one of being abandoned, I might interpret this experience with a belief that says, "I have been abandoned because there is something wrong with me and thus I am all alone." This thought will produce emotions such as insecurity, self-hate, fear of rejection and abandonment. When a new experience arises where I find myself alone again, I will begin with this same thinking and emotional response. I might say, "See, there is something wrong with me." Even if I learn new truth, such as, "God loves me and would never abandon me," it may have little or no impact on the original, experiential belief that "Since something is wrong with me I am all alone." Even though I may be able to quote the Scripture, "I am with you always" (Matt. 28:20) and yet still feel alone.

Problems arise for us when our new experiences are interpreted through the lens of older painful ones, which have nothing to do with the current experiences. The mind places the old interpretation over the top of the new experience and falsely interprets it. When this happens, the new experience will feel like the old, and we will react in the same way that we did in the original situation. This is the source of most relational conflict.

I said earlier that our beliefs about an event are what cause us painful emotions in the present; it is not the event itself. The event is over and the trauma is no longer happening, but the pain-laden beliefs remain. If the traumatic event was the reason we were still in pain, then theoretically we could never be free, since the memory of the event will always be present in the mind. The event, however, is merely the container, which holds the belief or interpretation that was given to the event. This is why each time anything occurs that is remotely similar to an earlier traumatic event, we feel the original pain. The present trigger simply activates the lie-based thinking in our memory, which produces emotion, which matches the belief, which usually results in poor and sinful choices. If I believe that I am dirty and shameful in a sexual abuse memory, then I will probably feel dirty and shameful when having sex with my marriage partner. I can logically know that I am not dirty during marital sex, yet still experience bad feelings if the lie-based memory is triggered by the present situation.

I remember watching the incest survivors in my group tremble in fear and abreact in pain as they revisited their memories of abuse. Some would gag and choke as though they were being orally raped. Why couldn't they tell themselves the truth and go on? Their minds were holding on to that which was no longer true. No amount of effort on their part or mine could free them from the power of the lies they believed. Only a word from the Spirit of Jesus Himself could free them.

Much Inappropriate Behavior Is Motivated by Lie-Based Pain

We are able to walk in freedom as we come into experiential truth from the Holy Spirit. This process is an intricate part of the total process of having our minds renewed. Discipleship, teaching and personal Bible study all play a part, but these things cannot accomplish this task on their own. The primary purpose of mind renewal is to remove the barriers of deception that hinder us from knowing and experiencing the truth of who and what we presently are, as a result of the total and complete work of Christ. Every lie we believe hinders our view of the truth of who we are in Christ. Every lie produces matching emotions, which cripple our life and walk with God. If we believe that we are worthless and no good, we will feel the same and in turn act out in a manner consistent with this belief.

When I was a child I received a lie that what I did was always less than what it should have been. As an adult, the emotions that this lie produced continually influenced my behavior. Some people who have accepted a similar lie become underachievers, feel defeated and give up on doing anything or are slow to attempt things.

I went in the opposite direction. I decided to prove that this was not true (even though I believed it was). Some might say that I did the right thing by choosing to try harder, accomplish more and prove the lie wrong. Yet all my diligent effort did not remove one sliver of the power of the lie. I just became driven and a workaholic, never accomplishing enough to alleviate the pain and ultimately forsaking my family.

My educational pursuit was a vain attempt to remove the pain caused by my lie-based thinking. I completed over one hundred hours of master's-level work in counseling and education and finished my Doctor of Ministry and most of the coursework for my Doctor of Education in marriage and family counseling before I began to discover the lies that were driving me. Today I no longer seem to be driven by these lies. Jesus has released me (for the most part) and my family and I are grateful. I'm not saying that educational degrees are not of value or importance, I am simply saying that not all good things are motivated by truth or peace. Much of what we do is driven by emotional pain or the avoidance thereof.

From my own personal experience and from watching those around me in ministry, I believe that much, if not most, of the ministry that is being performed in churches, pastor's offices and Christian counseling centers is motivated by people's pain more than by spirituality. I realize that I have just made a very big assumption and accusation, but let me explain.

I served in Southern Baptist churches for over 17 years before opening a private practice in pastoral counseling in the early 1990s. I operated this practice until 1995, when I burned out and then discovered and began using the Theophostic principles. During the first 20 years of my ministry I saw many good things happen in the lives of people with whom I ministered. People came to Christ, marriages were saved, and people became more spiritually and mentally functional and grew in knowledge and understanding of God and His Word. Yet as I look back at the emotion that was driving my work and ministry, I see underlying stress and anxiety. Some might see this as just a symptom of an A-type personality. However the truth is that a fear of rejection, a need for acceptance, feelings of inadequacy and a fear of people (to mention just a few of my lie-based emotions) were what drove my behavior. The lie-based pain contained in my childhood wounds was the primary motivation driving my ministry efforts. God used my efforts to help many people, but my motive was not one of peace. When I finally slowed things down and looked inside to see what was driving me, I found it was not the peace of Christ. There was a constant inner anxiety (rooted in lie-based thinking) that drove me like a task master. For the most part I was not even aware of this inner dynamic at work. I just went to work everyday and finally burned out.

Somewhere under all this pain I had a heartfelt desire for people and their renewal and growth, but my predominant driving force was lie-based pain. The difficult part of all of this it that I did not know that was so until I began to allow renewal to come into my own life through the principles in this book. I honestly believed that I was in good shape. I had already dealt with most of my life history (through denial and suppression), I had already forgiven those who had hurt me (willfully chosen to declare this) and I had a good grasp and understanding of what was going on inside of me (at least I thought so). I had for the most part, put my past behind me and was in good spiritual shape (ha). Those around me saw me as confident, in charge, determined, focused, spiritually mature, grounded in the Word and very well adjusted. I can now see that I presented most of these traits as a protection from further pain.

Over the last almost ten years I have had the privilege of meeting and talking with many hundreds of pastors, church leaders and Christian counselors who have shared basically the same journey that I have just described. What is exciting is that these church leaders are choosing to come clean and are seeking renewal and thus becoming more effective for the Kingdom. One thing I know to be true, it has taking much less energy admitting that I am a mess than it did to pretend and perform like I was not. It feels very good to be walking in more and more freedom and to know that the Lord will meet me in every place that I still need to visit.

What Is True Mind Renewal?

Mind renewal is both cognitive and experiential. Mind renewal goes beyond the gathering of biblical facts and knowledge to the place where the believer is able to experientially walk in the present reality of righteousness that he or she knows logically and has by faith laid hold of in Christ. Lie-based thinking robs us of knowing this reality. Though it is true "if any man is in Christ, he is a new creature" (2 Cor. 5:17) this truth reality does not always match our experiential reality. The reason that I do not always emotionally and experientially know this reality is often due in part to the lies I believe. Yet as each lie is replaced with truth, I come to know who and what I am in Christ, and this reality can become an effortless outflow of the truth I experientially possess.

The emotions that I feel that are contrary to what God says is true for me are either the consequence of wrong choices I have been deceived into making (sin), or else they are symptoms of my false self-belief and therefore not my true spiritual condition.

Christian growth and maturity is a revealing of what we possess in Christ Jesus. I am in Christ and what I was before (lost, depraved, separated from God) has all passed away (in my spirit), where "all things have become new" (2 Cor. 5:17, *NKJV*), whether or not I believe it, feel it or experientially know it. My lies tell me I am shameful, guilty, imperfect, less than others or unacceptable. God's Word says I am redeemed, righteous and holy. Who am I going to believe?

I am in the process of coming to the place where what I experientially believe matches what I am in Christ. Wherever there is deception and lies, I will have difficulty appropriating my present righteous place in Him.

Suffering Exposes Lie-Based Thinking

Some people have suggested that I am advocating a life free of *all* pain. This is not true. What I am saying is that any emotional pain that is rooted in faulty, lie-based thinking is not God's will for anyone at any time. However, it is God's will that Christians suffer as a result of life situations or as an overt act of persecution. Peter affirmed suffering as God's will when he said, "let those who suffer *according to the will of God* commit their souls to Him in doing good, as to a faithful Creator" (1 Pet.

4:19, *NKJV*, emphasis added). The apostle Paul said that he was destined to suffer for Christ (see 1 Thess. 3:3).

I am very aware and see the necessity of suffering in the life of the believer. As a matter of fact, suffering is a primary tool in the hand of God used for exposing my lie-based thinking. When the fire comes, I am exposed. If I know truth in my innermost part (not just logically and cognitively), I will remain in peace during the fire. If I believe lies, I will respond to the suffering through my lie-based thinking, and the painful emotions that match my belief will surface automatically. Paul's mind had been greatly renewed when he said, "I have learned to be content in whatever circumstances I am" (Phil. 4:11). James said that the proper response to suffering was joy, "Consider it all joy, my brethren, when you encounter various trials, knowing that the testing of your faith produces endurance, and let endurance have its perfect result so that you may be mature and complete lacking in nothing" (Jas. 1:2-3). Suffering exposes us and provides us an opportunity for mind renewal. This is the process that God has always operated within and Theophostic Prayer Ministry is an intentional decision to work in cooperation with Him.

Knowing the Peace of Christ

When what we believe at the experiential level matches the biblical truth we know at the logical level, we will walk in perfect peace. As long as we hold on to the lies of our experience, we will remain in a continual struggle between the lies we believe experientially and what we hold logically to be true. Paul said in Romans 12:2 that we need to be transformed in our behavior through the renewal of our minds. The next part of this verse tells us why, "That you may prove [manifest or live out] what the will of God is, that which is good and acceptable and perfect" (v. 3). God's perfect will is realized as we experientially come to know Him and experience genuine transformation through the renewing of our minds.

Ephesians 1:3-14 is a lengthy passage, but I want to encourage you to slowly read through what the apostle Paul is saying about our present condition and the relationship we possess in Christ. I have underlined some of the spiritual realities we presently possess and the tenses of the English verbs used in describing them. God wants us to experientially live in this reality, but our experiential lie-based thinking blinds the eyes of our heart from knowing these realities. I have not listed the entire passage in its fullness but have pulled out the primary aspects that I am wanting to emphasize. I encourage you to go back and sometime read it all. My comments appear within the brackets.

Blessed be the God and Father of our Lord Jesus Christ, who *has* [accomplished task] blessed us with *every* [nothing more to give] spiritual blessing in the heavenly places in Christ, just as He chose us in Him *before the foundation of the world*, [this was long before we had any say in the matter] that we should *be holy and blameless* before Him [God's plan from the beginning was that we have a holy relationship with Him] . . . In Him *we have* [present tense] *redemption through His* blood [completed task], the *forgiveness of our trespasses*, according to the riches of His grace, which He lavished upon us [fulfilled] . . . In Him also *we have obtained* [present tense] an inheritance, *having been* [past tense] predestined according to His purpose who works all things after the counsel of His will, . . . *you were sealed* [a done deal] in Him with the Holy Spirit of promise, who *is given* as a pledge of our inheritance, with a view to the redemption of God's own possession, to the praise of His glory (emphasis added).

After laying down this foundation, Paul goes on in verse 18 to declare the importance of having our minds renewed so that we might come to know these realities, "I pray that the eyes of your heart may be enlightened, so that you may know *what is* [present tense] the hope of His calling, *what are* [present tense] the riches of the glory of His inheritance in the saints" (emphasis added). As we find freedom from the lies stored in our memories, these truths can become an experiential reality.

This is why Paul declares in Romans 12:2 "be transformed [completely changed in behavior] by the renewing of your mind." Otherwise, we will have little choice but to be "conformed to the world" (v. 2). Until we are renewed in mind, we will never be able to know fully who we are in Christ. Every lie that God replaces with divine truth allows us to live more freely through our true present hearts of righteousness. As we come into the knowledge of who we are in Christ, we can appropriate the deeper things that result in the ongoing maturing of our inner person.

Experiential Knowledge and Logical Truth

Again, our memory contains at least two levels or types of information: logical truth and experiential knowledge. (Note that this is but one aspect of the complexities of memory). The logical data or truth is an accumulation of the information that we have gathered through non-experiential or non-emotional means and is emotionally passive. For example, we may gather biblical information sitting in a class lecture or sermon or from our personal Bible study. We might learn about the faithfulness of God and how He is our protector and the source of all things that we need in life. This information is true and has the potential to change our lives if we can experientially grasp it. We may even set out to apply this truth and discipline ourselves to do so. Nevertheless, this information is passively stored in our logical databases, apart from emotional experience. (Though the class setting is technically an experience, it does not usually require an emotional response or a personal interpretation.)

On the other hand, if later that night a mugger accosts us and robs us of all our money in a parking lot, we are gathering information that is experiential by nature. We might gather from this experience that God does not protect us, that this world is not a safe place and that we walk in constant danger of being hurt. The mugger incident gives us experiential knowledge that we may interpret in a fashion contrary to what we learned logically in Bible class. In the days ahead, as we walk across campus, we will likely feel fear, cautiousness and feelings of vulnerability, which come from our experiential knowledge. We might try to draw from our logical truth by quoting the passages of Scripture about God's protection, but we may still feel fear. Because we have learned this information experientially, our minds may rely more heavily on it than on the logical truth we learned in the classroom setting.

In like manner, when emotionally charged events occurred in our childhood, we interpreted them from the emotions we felt. These interpretations became our basic and guiding source of information for any future situation that was even remotely similar.

We can choose to embrace logical truth in times of crisis, but generally we will submit to that which we feel is true rather than that we know to be true. This is why people who administer Theophostic Prayer Ministry ask the person undergoing ministry what feels true, as opposed to what is true when looking for the lie. What we feel is an indication of what we experientially believe. If we are in a non-threatening environment like a Sunday school class, we will spout off the logical truth we have memorized. This truth is not necessarily what we operate from when we are in a real-life situation.

As I mentioned earlier as a way of example, if we lose our jobs next week our feelings will expose our true beliefs. If we are overcome with panic, fear and uncertainty, then we do not experientially believe that "God shall supply all your needs" (Phil. 4:19), even though we have the verse memorized. What we feel shows what we experientially believe. Our experiences dictate, for the most part, how we will act in the present. If we have lies embedded in our life memory experiences, we may be crippled in our perception and life choices.

Those who have suffered childhood trauma clearly show how one's experiential knowledge dictates one's present reality. If you have worked with survivors of sexual abuse, then the following scenario will be very familiar to you.

Janice was washing dishes when her husband came up behind her and gave her a gentle hug. Immediately she recoiled and reacted negatively to his embrace. In anger she scolded him not to do that. He was confused by her reaction, since all he had done was hug her. She could not explain why she reacted this way, but nevertheless she did not like what he had done. What happened? Janice's mind supplied her with experiential knowledge of past abuse. She felt the emotion and sensation of being held against her will, which she had learned in the childhood abuse. Logical truth could tell her she was presently safe and that her husband's hug was good, yet her experiential knowledge hindered her from receiving and embracing the reality of this truth.

As Christians, we need logical truth in order to grow and mature in the Christian life, but this truth is difficult to appropriate if our experiential knowledge is contrary. If we believe the lie that says, "I am stupid and cannot do anything right," we will have great difficulty receiving and living out the truth that we are loved and accepted by God. Our emotional responses to life situations will match our experiential belief system, not our logical database. It does not matter what we say or think we believe, because our emotions will expose our true belief systems when we are faced with real-life situations. What we believe to be true in a given situation will be evident by what we feel in that moment. If we say that we believe God supplies all our needs and is our Protector, yet we experience fear or anxiety in a given situation, then we really experientially believe something different from this. Due to this conflict between logical beliefs and experiential knowledge, many of us struggle to live out our logical truth. Our logical data tells us that we are forgiven and that God accepts and loves us, but our experiential knowledge often condemns us.

Joan came to me depressed and with much body pain, which she could find no physical explanation. I asked her if there were times when she felt more pain and depression than others, and she reported that she felt more pain at work than anywhere else. She said that she loved her work but that at the same time it depressed her. I asked her about her job and discovered that she was part of a ministry for unwed mothers in a pregnancy crisis center. I asked her to feel the emotional pain she felt at her ministry, and then asked her if she was willing to look to see where this pain might be rooted. Almost immediately she said, "But I have already dealt with that. I know that God forgave me for that!" Joan had had an abortion as a teenager, and had asked the Lord for His forgiveness while seeking counseling from a pastor many years before. So I asked her what she felt as she looked at the abortion memory. She began to sob, and said, "I feel so ashamed. But I know God has forgiven me. I just cannot understand why I still feel so bad. I guess I just cannot forgive myself."[1] Joan's logical truths about God's forgiveness and grace were right on target, but this had had little effect on her emotional state.

This scenario is common with people who have sinned in dramatic ways. They have sought genuine forgiveness and yet cannot find release from the pain. What was happening here was a conflict between what Joan's logical truth was saying and what her experiential knowledge was telling her. I asked Joan to embrace the pain she was feeling and to discern why she was feeling what she was feeling. She said, "I feel like a murderer. I killed my baby. How can God ever forgive me? But I know I am forgiven. I have confessed this terrible sin a hundred times and have asked Him to forgive me. Why can't I go on? Why do I still feel such shame?"

Years ago I would have pulled out my "Claim it by faith," "Reckon it to be so" and "Trust God, not your feelings" lectures. Today I said, "Let yourself feel the shame and embrace the thought that you are a murderer." I then continued with the Theophostic process and watched as the Spirit of Jesus began to experientially minister to Joan with truth. In just a few minutes she looked up at me with a changed countenance, beaming with joy and release. She said through her tears, "He just said it was really okay. I am forgiven." Now Joan's experience matched her logical truth and thus was able to walk in effortless victory in this area of her life. In the past she had had to battle the shameful feelings and claim the truth even though it did not feel true. Now she could claim the truth and experience the peace and joy this truth afforded. By the way, Joan's body pain never returned after this session. The body often expresses the conflict in our thinking through physical pains and ailments. When our minds are at peace, our bodies frequently will heal themselves. When there is lie-based pain in our minds, our bodies often act out accordingly. I believe this is why we don't see more physical healing in the church today. When physical illness is rooted in lie-based thinking it will not go away until the lies are removed. If my headaches are rooted in my lie-based thinking, God would not likely heal my headache which is but a symptom. Yet He can give me experiential truth, and as a natural result my headache should go away on its own.

Change Experience with Experience

We can change data with data, but it requires experience to change experience.

People come to counselors and ministers for help for many reasons, but mostly they come for help with emotional pain. They may say they've come because of what is happening in their lives, but the bottom line is they feel bad. Almost always the reason for the presenting pain is partly rooted in historical lie-based thinking. Remember, we are not usually miserable or in pain because of what has happened to us, but because of how we have interpreted what has happened. When true renewal occurs in a person's mind, the memories of painful events will still be intact, but the lies will no longer be attached to the memories, and consequently the pain associated with those memories will also be gone. Lies such as "I am bad, no good, not lovable, rejected, abandoned, shameful, evil and so on" cause us to feel bad, not what has happened to us. What we believe about what happened is what causes the pain.

Many counselors seek to change wrong beliefs by providing those they counsel with Scriptures or truth statements. To the degree that the thinking is logical or misinformation, change can occur. For example if I believed that Moses built the ark to cross the Red Sea, new information could set me straight. But if my misinformation is emotionally charged you may find it difficult to effect much change by simply telling me the truth. Some people expect the wounded person to hear and receive the truth and then quit thinking the false thoughts and thereby feel better. Yet if we are honest, we know that this does not work very well. People may leave our office encouraged and determined to feel better but usually return with the same pain when something happens that stirs it back up again.

Sharon and I were on a trip to the Chicago area one day. We left our home in central Kentucky, taking Interstate I-65, which runs north and south. For those of you who may not know, Chicago, Illinois, is north of Kentucky, while Tennessee is the state that lies due south. Once we got on I-65, I set the cruise control, relaxed and enjoyed conversing with my wife as we headed for Chicago. After a couple of hours, Sharon asked me, "Are you sure we are going the right direction?"

I responded as any red-blooded male would answer, "Say what? Of course, I know where we are."

After traveling a hundred miles down the road, an extremely large and boisterous sign proclaimed the words, "Welcome to Tennessee."

In the above scenario my misinformation was immediately changed by this road sign. Or if I am still not swayed by the revelatory information I could pull out my map and see the (logical) truth of how to get to my destination, I will immediately assume that the former directions were false and make the necessary corrections. This correction is immediately stored in my logical database, where I can avoid the same mistake, should I ever pass that way again. This logical adjustment is easy to make in this area of the mind (except for having to face my wife with my mistake), since this simply requires me to change data with data. However, had my wife said something such as, "I thought you said you knew where you were going?" I would have probably felt small, inadequate, stupid and a sundry of other painful emotions and then covered it all over with a defensive and angry response. The lies that would have been exposed in that moment would have not easily been resolved by someone telling me that I was smart, capable, God's creation, loved, etc. I would have needed to go to the source of this pain and expose my thinking to the Lord Himself.

In contrast, however, it's not so easy to change what we believe experientially. More often than not, if you give a person new information that conflicts with what is stored in his or her experiential knowledge, that person will not even acknowledge the new information. He or she will subconsciously filter out the new information, since it does not match what is experientially believed.

Janice was a member of an incest survivors group I used to oversee before I began doing Theophostic Prayer Ministry. I used support groups to allow people with like problems to struggle together. This gave them a sense of not being alone.

Janice came each week to the group very depressed. She rarely fixed herself up before coming. Her hair was usually pulled back and her clothes seldom matched. Yet one night she came to group with her hair fixed up and a new outfit on. I immediately noticed and made a complimentary comment. Janice did not even look in my direction. I repeated myself, and she looked at me and gave me a very weak and cynical "thank you." I reassured her that I had meant what I had said, but I could see that she did not receive my words, so I asked her why she could not accept my compliment. She said, "I know that you really don't mean it." However, I did mean it, so I asked her how she had felt when I said the nice words to her. She gave me a strange look and said, "I know that what I am thinking is not true, but what I think is that you want sex. Men talk nice to me only when they want something."

Here is a good example of how one's experiential knowledge overrides incoming logical truth. This is why a preacher can deliver a powerful, truth-filled sermon that leaves his or her congregation neither touched nor changed. Perhaps we put the proverbial cart before the horse when we try to help people grow spiritually by filling their cart with more logical truth than their experiential horse can pull.

Go to the Gospels and read the stories of Jesus healing people. See how often He provided them an experience before He gave them the truth. Jesus healed the blind man without even talking to him first. Later, after the religious leaders in the temple had rejected the former blind man, he was given logical data about the identity of his Healer. Here the man with restored sight heard the truth from Jesus and believed Him to be the Messiah who had come (see John 9:32-33). I am not sure which must come first, the chicken or the egg, but I do know that logical truth and experience must both be present in a person's life in order for genuine change to occur. Biblical truth without a genuine experience of God is powerless in bringing about genuine change.

Information that is emotionally stored in my experience will require a new experience to change it. This can happen only when the lie-based memory is replaced with experiential truth. Only the Holy Spirit can provide experiential truth to my historical experience. When the Holy Spirit reveals to the wounded person, "You are not alone," that person's experience changes. If I had told that person, "You are not alone; God is with you," he or she would have agreed logically but probably still felt rejected. If we believe we are stupid and incompetent in our experience, very little new information will have an impact on what we have embraced as true. We can take a difficult test, score 100 percent on it and we'll assume the test was flawed. If our friends and associates tell us over and over how competent we are, we will still feel just the opposite. Logical data has little power over what our experiences have taught us, yet many counseling offices, as well local church ministries, often try to change our experiential lie-based thinking with such data.

The Problem With the 4-P Approach to Ministry

Most churches pray for people who come for prayer during an altar call, and often the one praying speaks words of encouragement and truths from the Bible. This is a fine thing to do. However, these prayers do not always result in a changed life. For the most part people return to their seats with the same emotional pain that they had when they came forward. Does this mean that prayer is ineffective in this context? Absolutely not! We must pray. However, I believe that prayer that does not address the core issues of a person's life will fall short in its effectiveness. In this context we often make the mistake of trying to change experience with logical truth alone.

As an example, I offer the following. It was a typical Sunday morning service at our church. We had experienced a good time of praise and worship and heard an insightful message, and the minister had asked people to come forward if they desired personal ministry. Several came forward and shared their needs with the pastor. Each one shared similar concerns, which pertained to some difficulty in their present life, accompanied by a measure of obvious emotional pain. The pastor, in turn, asked for people from the congregation to come forward to pray with those who had asked for ministry. A number of people answered the call of the pastor, and soon prayers began to flow for those who had confessed their need. After a season of prayer the people all returned to their seats and the service drew to a close. I believe it was assumed by most people present that those who came for prayer were now in a better place spiritually and emotionally as a result of the prayers prayed by their fellow members. After the prayer time, they appeared to be less troubled and showed signs of being comforted and grateful for the expressions of concern that were offered.

As I watched the scene play out, I wondered what had really occurred in this common scenario. Did the emotional pain these people were feeling go away as a result of the prayer time? Did they go back to their seats renewed and in a different place than before the prayers were offered? What would they say to me if I asked them if the prayers had actually resulted in genuine release of their pain and the presence of perfect peace?

Based on my own experience of being prayed for and on the answers to these very questions that I've received from people who have received prayers for their emotional pains, I have found that not much change usually occurs. Too often we may feel better initially because of the affirmation and comfort we receive from others, but by the time we get to the parking lot, we are in the same place of pain we were before we went forward for prayer.

Does this mean that prayer does not work, is unnecessary or is impotent? No, prayer does work—when it is applied within the proper context and in biblically supportive applications. Nevertheless, if these people are not truly helped through the prayers we pray, then why do we pray for them? It could be because we do not know what else to do. In any other area of life, work or business, when what we are doing doesn't produce a desirable outcome, we reevaluate the practice, seek alternative approaches and continue to try new things until we achieve the results we desire. Yet, people in the church often do the same things over and over, with little or no result, and make changes only as a last resort, and then rarely without the shedding of much blood.

Over the last 20 years there has been a new effort by many pastors and ministers to go beyond praying and become trained in counseling. Most seminaries now offer degrees in counseling. However, many ministers who have tried their hand at counseling find the trade-off costly, due to the enormous amount of time invested for often feeble results. Others have come to the conclusion (after many hours of working with the same people on the same issues, with little to show for their efforts) that counseling produces about as much fruit as trying to pray people's pain away. Most churches default to what I call the 4-P approach to ministry, which is problem-pray-pretend-perform. It works like this: The person comes to the church with a *problem* or an emotional pain, which the church attempts to resolve through *prayer*. Once the prayers are offered up, the recipient is expected to *pretend* to be better by smiling, being grateful and saying that he or she is better (when he or she usually is not). Then the person melds back into the congregational mold of *performance*-based spirituality.[2] If the person cannot pretend and perform, he or she is then labeled by the church as unwilling to be healed, a carrier of some hidden sin he or she is unwilling to confess, not really saved or maybe even demonized.

If a person is considered demonized (the commonly assumed reason that the prayer was ineffective), some ministers apply the 4-P+D approach, which adds *deliverance* from the demon to the mix. It might be assumed that the demon must be battled and cast out before the person can be free. Yet casting out a demon does not make a person any freer of lie-based thinking than he or she was before, just a little demon-less. In most cases when a person comes for prayer for his or her pain and struggles, that person will simply default to suppression of the pain, pretending relief and performance for at least the amount of time it takes to get to his or her car in the parking lot.

I would like to suggest that we are taking the wrong approach, at least in part. I am not saying that we should not pray for each other, for we must. However, we should look to the Scriptures and see how we are to pray, under what circumstances, and for what purposes, rather than using prayer as a fix-all approach to ministry. Maybe God doesn't intend for us to pray our pain and difficulties away. Maybe He wants us to find the true source of our emotional pain, face it and embrace it, and in this context discover His truth and lasting freedom. Theophostic Prayer Ministry is a specific and focused prayer approach that seeks to encourage people to discover the true sources of their pain and allows them to encounter Jesus.

As I sat in church that morning, watching those who had come forward for prayer, I was reminded of a poor fellow who was rushed to the hospital with acute appendicitis. He was in really bad shape. The church was alerted and the prayer team was sent in. They prayed for several hours over the man but his condition worsened.

After a few more hours his appendix ruptured and his prognosis became grim. A second prayer team was called in, and they prayed fervently all the way up to the moment of the man's death. Since he was now in a better place (heaven), those praying assumed it must not have been God's will for this man to be healed. After all, they had done all they could do (pray). Can you see the problem in this story? The man had appendicitis! There is a common cure for the condition; it's called surgery. He did not have to die, since an appendectomy is a simple procedure (at least this is what I am told). A surgeon could have been called in, made an incision, cut out the infected part and thereby removed the source of the illness. I am afraid that the church spends many hours praying for the healing of "appendicitis" when what we need is God's scalpel.

Some of you may be offended by my suggestion that there are applications where prayer alone is inadequate and exorcism is incomplete. Please don't misunderstand me. I am not saying that prayer is ineffective. Prayer is a vitally important biblical directive that we must do in the overall scope of ministry. Furthermore, I am not saying that exorcism is not a necessary part of a person's total ministry need, when indeed it is called for and when a person is truly demonized. I have on rare occasions watched people being prayed for come into complete peace as the Spirit of God moved in powerful ways, releasing them of the pain and struggles in their lives without anything other than prayer being applied. I also believe this only happened because the person encountered the Lord at their point of pain.

However, much of the time people who receive prayer for emotional renewal and help may feel loved and encouraged, but they remain in pain. I hope that we can make an honest appraisal of the outcome of the ministry we offer wounded people. Are people permanently moving from pain to peace in the areas of their lives for which they come to the church for help? We, as a church, have sometimes misinformed the wounded when we have communicated that if they would come with their pain and allow us to pray, things would get better. We may not actually say these words, but if our response to others' troubles and pain is merely praying them through to victory, we may be forcing them to apply the 4-P method of relief.

Who Needs Emotional Renewal?

People often ask me how many people I think are in need of emotional renewal. My answer is, "Everyone raise your right hand." All of us need emotional renewal and mind renewal. Not one of us is exempt. We all have lies in our thinking and minds that need to be renewed.

As I have already said, it is not a question of who needs ministry and renewal, but to what extent we need it and how extensive the damage is. We are all emotionally wounded, but in varying degrees. Every person sitting in every church everywhere (in the pews and behind the pulpit) carries emotional pain at some level. You might think that you are okay and that you do not have any lie-based thinking. You may not have been abused or hurt in any significant manner as a child, and may even have been raised in a warm, loving and spiritual home. Nevertheless, you have not made it this far without picking up lies.

Think over the last few weeks. Were there any moments in which you were frustrated, stressed, angered, worried, anxious, taxed, upset, fearful, hateful, argumentative, defeated or pressured? If so, there was probably a lie at the source of these emotions. You may argue that you had a right to feel this way, or that your feelings were normal reactions to the situation. Yet the Bible is clear that we are to be ruled by the peace of Christ. We are told to be "anxious for nothing" (Phil. 4:6). Nothing does not leave much room for anything else. If we feel an absence of His peace, we are not walking in truth. What if you could have faced those same life experiences and felt peaceful rather than stirred? You can—if you choose to look inward and allow the Spirit of Christ to reveal to you His truth.

Some believe that good behavior equals spiritual maturity and that keeping our pain hidden (even from ourselves) is a virtue. Everywhere I go, I find the church is basically the same: a building with many emotionally wounded people trying hard to pretend that everything is well. Many of us sing, "It is well with my soul" (and indeed it is in our new hearts), but our minds are in pain. We stand and proclaim "Victory in Jesus" and "Standing on the Promises," while we live in secret defeat and emotional bondage. We call abstinence from sinning victory, when it is not. At some level we all need release from the lies we believe.

Emotionally wounded people can be healed and can find peace and freedom — but not everyone who needs renewal is lining up for his or her portion. I have worked with people who knew they were in pain and claimed they knew the reason for the pain yet never sought release. They chose to hold on to a lie that said the reason for their pain was due to outside sources (people, situations, etc.) and an unwillingness to look inward.

Ann came to me complaining of a troubled marriage. She said she had already filed for divorce and had no plans of stopping the process. The only reason she had come for ministry that day was out of respect for her husband's last request before she ended the marriage. She told him she would come one time, but did not plan on coming a second time. I asked her what she felt the trouble was in their relationship.

I was surprised by her response. She said she had a good husband. He was more than she could have ever wanted or asked for. He was attentive to her every need, he was romantic, he talked to her and he paid careful attention to family matters. She had only one complaint. She said that every time he came near her sexually, it made her skin crawl. She felt overwhelmed and trapped. She did not feel it was fair to him for them to go on in this manner, and wanted a divorce.

I asked her to focus on the feeling she felt when her husband approached her sexually. Her face began to contort with disgust. I asked her to disconnect from the picture of her and her husband but to stay focused on the painful emotion that had surfaced. Then I asked the Lord to help her find the place where she had felt this same emotional pain for the first time. All of the sudden she opened her eyes with a startled look on her face.

I asked her what she was remembering. With some resistance she finally shared the painful story. The problem was not her dislike of sex, or what her husband was doing with her sexually. Her unhappiness with sex came from lies, which had been planted during sexual abuse years earlier. The lies from her history had infiltrated what could have been a very happy and healthy marriage. However, as is sometimes the case, this woman left the session unwilling to deal with her memory, face the lies and chose not to believe that these feelings toward her husband could be from her past. She made the decision to leave the marriage. The last report I had from her was that the same issues had surfaced in her new relationship. The new man in her life triggered the same pain, because the pain was not in the relationship but in her lie-based memories.

This story underlines the necessity of embracing the emotional pain of our lives. We can bury the memory, but its pain will eventually surface, causing more problems. I have no doubt that if this woman could have embraced the reality of the abuse in her life, felt its pain and received truth from the Spirit of Christ, she would have experienced His perfect peace and saved her marriage.

If your marriage is in trouble, I have hope for you. However, it will require you to stop blaming your spouse and be willing to go to the original places of your pain. If you are willing to do this, Christ can meet you there and you can find His perfect peace and release.

For whatever reason, most people believe that counseling or ministry is only for those deeply troubled. If you are seeing a counselor or minister, you may be seen as one of those who just cannot get it together on your own. I hope that what I am writing in this book helps to tear down this falsehood and opens the door for all people to begin a healing or mind renewal journey. We are all lie-infested in some measure and in need of release.

I want to encourage you to slow down a bit and become emotionally aware throughout your day. Notice when and what stirs you up emotionally in negative ways. What is it your spouse says or does that gets to you? What is it about your work that causes you to feel bad? Too often we just respond from our pain, while we instantly justify our pain-driven behavior. We are called to walk in inner peace. Peace is a natural by-product of experientially knowing truth. You feel what you believe: When you know truth in your innermost parts, you will have the perfect peace of Christ.

Chapter Five

When God Renews the Mind . . .

Are People Really Being Renewed?

Perhaps you're wondering, How can I know for sure that people are truly finding release and renewal through this method? Can real recovery from traumatic memory be lifted as has been suggested? How do I know it will last? How do I even know if the memories people are reporting are true? How can I be certain that what is happening through Theophostic Prayer Ministry is truly of God? Before we explore these questions more fully, let's reflect on the reasons they are raised in the first place.

Early on, no one questioned the validity of this ministry more than I did. I was skeptical, even though I was standing in the middle of what I am now convinced was God doing the miraculous. Over and over I witnessed God help the emotionally lame and blind to walk and to see. I saw people consistently come to a place of rest in the presence of Jesus as He revealed His truth into their pain-filled memories. My limited view and experience could not comprehend this. I wondered if the changes I witnessed would last, if this method could be transferred to other counselors and ministers and if it could be applied outside the context of what I was doing in other fields of ministry. Could I be certain that God was the source of the messages the people were apparently receiving? I had always believed (logical data) that God could do miracles in the world today, yet I was having trouble with Him doing them in my own life and ministry. Miracles were something God did on special occasions—not every day.

I was seeing people find genuine peace in their places of pain. People were finding true release, session by session, as they were receiving His truth. As I continued to witness what seemed to be instantaneous recovery from lies rooted in painful memories in a person's life, I slowly let go of my skepticism and began to embrace what has become for me a very reliable and effective ministry tool.

I was seeing people enter into perfect peace, draw closer to God and experience Jesus in a real and meaningful way. How could this be deception?

Simon was sexually abused at the age of five by his father. The abuse occurred only once, yet it left deep wounds of shame and confusion in this young man's life. During his first session with me, we discovered two lies that had been implanted in his mind during the abuse: *I am dirty and shameful for allowing my dad to touch me,* and *I am bad because I waited so long after the fact to report it.* I led this young man through Theophostic Prayer Ministry, and he immediately reported complete peace as he received healing truth from God. All the shame and guilt were gone. The next week he returned for his second session. We began by looking again at the original memory of abuse. I asked him to look for anything that did not feel completely peaceful and calm. I watched as he searched through the memory, looking for pain. He found none. The pain, shame and guilt were still gone. Halfway through the session, he asked if we could end the session early because he had other things he needed to do. Emotionally crippled the week before, he now claimed he was completely free of the pain with which he had come in.

If I had met Simon before I developed Theophostic Prayer Ministry, I likely would have worked with him for years as I tried to get him to restructure his thinking and habitual behaviors and learn to manage the emotional pain. No longer. It has been my experience that when a person receives truth in his or her lie-based memories, that person's dysfunctional patterns simply go away. This is really not all that difficult to understand, if indeed the dysfunctional behaviors are the person's attempt to deal with his or her pain. Remember, sin patterns, compulsions, addictive behaviors and other disorders are usually people's solutions for pain rather than their problems. For example, if you came to me for ministry as a person suffering from an eating disorder, such as anorexia, I would not try to get you to start eating. I could tell you that if you did not eat, you would die, but you would already know this. I could tell you that you were skin and bones, but you would not believe me. If I tried to make you eat, you would resist me, since refraining from eating was your solution and not your perceived problem.[1] Somehow you have determined that by not eating you can thereby manage your emotional pain. For example, if your pain is the feelings of being out of control, not eating might give you a sense of being in control.

I might ask how it made you feel to think about eating a meal, and then I might describe the potatoes, gravy and roast beef and ask you how my description made you feel. This usually stirs up the very emotions that the anorexia is masking or seeking to resolve. You might tell me, "To eat makes me feel out of control," or, "I feel afraid, powerless, angry and helpless." Yet once the lies producing these emotions are removed, the need for the solution will probably go away. When you know the truth, experientially, you should no longer need your solution and can let go of the disorder.

When Archie came to see me, he had no apparent disorder. His parents hadn't abused him as a child and he'd not experienced any serious trauma, yet he was still in emotional pain. He was suffering from daily anxiety over his finances. He had come to me the year before I began using Theophostic Prayer Ministry, and we had logically worked through his financial situation, showing him that he had no reason to fear yet his fears remained. I had thought the information I had provided would calm the fear and enable him to move on with his life. It didn't. In fact, when he came to see me again, he said his anxiety was worse than it had been the year before.

Like all of us, Archie carried a variety of lie-based thoughts that he had picked up throughout childhood. Archie experienced an incredible amount of renewal during his first Theophostic Prayer Ministry session with me, and came back for a follow-up session the following week. In this session he excitedly reported that he had experienced no anxiety over his finances all week. He could no longer access his fear over finances. No matter how hard he tried to surface the fear and anxiety, he could not.

As I mentioned earlier, in the beginning I was very skeptical of what was happening during these Theophostic Prayer Ministry sessions. I came up with four questions to help me discern whether God was doing a work of renewal in a person who had received Theophostic Prayer Ministry.

1. Is the message received from God during the session biblically consistent?

2. Does the person demonstrate the presence of the perfect peace of Christ in the memory that has been renewed?

3. Does the person have genuine compassion and forgiveness for those who have hurt him or her concerning the specific memory event?

4. Is there evidence of life transformation as a result of the mind renewal?

Is the Message Biblically Consistent?

The truth the person reports receiving must be tested and challenged for biblical consistency. The Spirit of Christ will not give a message that is contrary or additional to what has already been given in the Scriptures. This is not to say that the message will always be a direct quote from Scripture, but the message will not conflict with Scripture or add to it.

For example, a person might report hearing the Lord say, "You are not alone. I am here with you," in a memory of a time when he or she had been abandoned. These words are consistent with Jesus' words: "I am with you always, even to the end of the age" (Matt. 28:20). If the message received is not consistent with Scripture, then it is not valid. This "truth" should be rejected because it is not from God.

One day I was working with a woman who was reporting a memory of her father beating her mother. She saw herself hiding behind a table, watching helplessly, in terror of what was happening. She was fearful that her mother was going to be killed and that she would be all alone, without protection from her dad. The mother did not die and the father never hurt this woman as a child, yet she still felt this fear. I asked the Lord Jesus to reveal to her His truth, and she told me, "He said that it was okay for me to be afraid. He also said for me not to think about this anymore. He said I should think about the good things my father did and put this memory behind me." I believed that this message was a falsehood and challenged it. This message violates Scripture. God's Word says, "perfect love casts out fear" (1 John 4:18). Therefore, it is not "okay to be afraid." Furthermore, not thinking about such things is denial.

Messages that are contrary to biblical truth may come from the person's own thoughts and conclusions. Other times they may originate from deceiving spirits who are seeking to confuse or hinder the renewal. A person administering Theophostic Prayer Ministry must discern the validity of the reported message. This is why the minister must "be diligent to present [himself] approved to God as a workman who does not need to be ashamed, handling accurately the word of truth" (2 Tim.

2:15). To be effective, the minister must be biblically knowledgeable and growing daily in God's Word.

Andrew came to me defeated in his Christian life due to his addiction to pornography on the Internet. He had struggled for years with lust and with impulses to buy pornographic magazines, but with free access to hundreds of thousands of hard-core pornographic web sites, most of the time he gave in to his impulse. Andrew was part of a support ministry that helped him abstain from his addiction, but he told me that his mind was tormented with flashes and images of what he had already experienced.

Theophostic Prayer Ministry addresses pornography addiction differently than do some other approaches, because it doesn't see addiction to pornography as the root problem, but as the person's solution for lie-based pain. Some ministries see pornography solely as a sin problem that needs to be confessed, repented of and somehow overcome. The truth is that this latter approach has had little success, since it is based on self-effort and willpower.

Andrew was trying to solve his emotional pain by calming and distracting it with pornography. Genuine freedom would never be found in self-sustained abstinence. He was surprised when I told him this. I explained to him that in order to find genuine release he must first identify what was driving the behavior (emotional pain) and then follow this pain back to its true source. When the memory source was discovered, the next step would be to discern what was believed in the memory that was producing the pain and then to allow Jesus to reveal His truth to Andrew in the memory.

I asked Andrew what he felt just prior to going to his computer to view the pornography. I was not surprised when he told me he felt sexually aroused. However, I did not assume that this was the primary feeling that was driving the behavior. The sexual arousal he felt was his solution to his pain. So I asked Andrew to think about what he felt just prior to feeling sexual arousal. He thought for a moment, but eventually he began to tear up. With a trembling voice he began to speak of deep pain of abandonment and rejection he had felt since early childhood. We asked the Lord Jesus to help Andrew to discover the first time he had felt these same deep, painful feelings. We soon ended up in painful childhood experiences, and here we discerned the lies behind Andrew's pain and invited Jesus to release him of this bondage.

Andrew began to hear a deceptive message, which he assumed was from the Spirit of Christ, "You must battle this problem, but if you do not give up you will win." This may sound noble, but it isn't biblically consistent. We do not have to battle sin. Jesus took on our sins on our behalf so that we could become free from sin.

This was probably a message from a demonic spirit trying to keep Andrew in the cycle of defeat (defeat-confess-repent-adjust-perform). This lie was exposed and rejected, and soon Andrew received biblically consistent truth from the Holy Spirit, which released him of his emotional pain and resulted in true peace. After a few more sessions and many painful memories, Andrew reported release from the strong desire to view pornography. Remember, true freedom and victory require no effort on our part to maintain.[2] Andrew said that he found it easy to abstain from pornography when the pain was removed, since he really did not want to do it anyway.

Another time, a person reported to me that God said that the reason she was feeling so badly was because she had been sexually abused. She received this message prior to having surfaced any memories that suggested such was the case. I suggested that what she had heard was not truth but a deception of some kind. I never accept this sort of message as being from God, because God does not tell us the content of our memories apart from our own self-discovery. Instead, He allows us to uncover them as we have the capacity and the willingness to embrace them. Whenever a person reports that God has told them something that is not in line with their choosing (such as revealing the content of a memory) I assume it is deception. Otherwise such would be a violation of our will. People remember painful memories when they are willing and able, not because God makes them.

Memory is a very complex process and far beyond the scope of Theophostic Prayer Ministry to completely explain. However, in this context it is important to realize that it is the interpretation of the memory event (however accurate or inaccurate it may be) that causes us trouble more so than the event itself. This can be especially true if the memory holding the false interpretation is not readily available to the conscious mind. Sometimes children choose to protect themselves by putting painful events in mental places where they do not have to access them with their conscious minds. This is an intentional and deliberate ignoring of memory information (though initially consciously performed and then subconsciously maintained) that allows them to deny the event and therefore suppress the emotional pain stored in the event. If it never happened then I do not have to feel it.

There are some people who suggest that any memory that is not consciously accessible is therefore not a true memory but rather false and must have been implanted by the minister or counselor. There is a long history of research that says otherwise. Nevertheless, a wise minister is careful to never make any suggestion of what he or she might think may be contained in someone else's memory (see the Ministry Session Guidelines at the end of this book). When we are ready to know the truth of what has happened to us, we will remember to the degree that we need to in order to find release of the lies contained therein.

Does the Person Demonstrate the Perfect Peace of Christ?

If a person has received truth from Christ in his or her lie-based memory, God's perfect peace will always be present. The apostle Paul taught "let the peace of Christ rule in your hearts" (Col. 3:15). Peace always follows the Holy Spirit's message of truth. Lies steal our peace, while truth is the basis for our peace.

A person who administers Theophostic Prayer Ministry seeks to encourage a person to discern the lies they have believed so that they might discover the truth that Christ has for them, resulting in His perfect peace. Such peace rarely, if ever, comes simply because the minister gives the wounded person truth in a logical instructive context though this is possible. If cognitive truth always resulted in peace, our churches would be full of peace-filled people. Christians today have more truth than any generation in the history of the Church, yet many do not walk in perfect peace. A lack of peace indicates that there is a lie present. Peace follows when lies are replaced with God's truth.

If a person reports what appears to be biblically consistent truth and yet the pain remains and peace continues to be elusive, I've found that this truth is probably coming from the person's logical database of truth. Again, when the truth is experientially provided by the Holy Spirit, it will bring about genuine release of lie-based thinking. Freedom is a God-initiated and God-accomplished task, "For it is God who is at work in you, both to will and to work for His good pleasure" (Phil. 2:13).

Some may think I am minimizing preaching, biblical instruction and personal Bible study. This is not the case. All I am saying is that it is the Holy Spirit who leads us into *all* truth. We may hear a spiritually rich sermon but unless the Holy Spirit implants this truth experientially into our heart and mind, it is only recorded as data and logical information. We may study the Scriptures daily but unless the Holy Spirit interprets them and teaches us we will only become more biblically smart.

Theophostic Prayer Ministry is a systematic means of helping people to position themselves at the feet of Jesus so He might do all He has promised. In a sense, it is helping people to listen. "He who has ears to hear, let him hear" (Matt. 11:15; Mark 4:9; Luke 8:8, 14:35).

Does the person have genuine compassion and forgiveness for those who have hurt him or her concerning the specific memory event?

Before I started doing Theophostic Prayer Ministry, I would work people through their mental barriers, appeal to Scripture, have them push through their anger and other revengeful emotions, and lead them through my formula prayer of forgiveness. After the prayer I would have them claim by faith that they had forgiven their offender, even though they often did not feel differently. Even those that did have an experience by praying the prayer with me usually had difficulty later.

For example, a fellow came to me who hated his father for the bad things done to him when he was a child. I showed him what the Bible said concerning forgiveness, and led him to confess his hate and to choose to forgive his father. He did, and was relieved until the family reunion a few months later, when he saw his father. As soon as his father walked into the room, this man felt a wave of resentment surface.

Did he really forgive his father? Or did he just need to claim forgiveness by faith, deny his feelings and act out the truth? I believe that he did forgive his father (to the measure he was able), but the resentment surfaced because he had not dealt with the true source of his pain, which was lie-based thinking held in memory. He lacked peace not from being unwilling to forgive but because he hadn't identified the lies producing the pain and received Christ's freedom in truth. Forgiveness releases a debt, but does not always release us from our lie-based emotion.

Since I began using the Theophostic Prayer Ministry model, I have watched person after person genuinely forgive those who have offended them as a result of the truth and peace they receive during a ministry session. Forgiveness is a natural by-product of receiving personal release from lie-based pain. When people truly find release of their lie-based pain, forgiveness and compassion for their offenders are natural outcomes.

I remember a young woman in her mid 20s who was emotionally devastated from being raped a few years earlier. This event had taken her emotionally out of commission and was ruining her life. The man showed no regard for her life and repeatedly threatened to kill her if she ever told what had happened. She was filled with terror and with rage and bitterness toward the rapist.

During a session with me, she was willing to revisit the rape memory. Hate, anger, rage, fear, shame and feelings of abandonment surfaced. We identified many different lies that she had attached to the memory, such as, "The rape was my fault," "I should have told someone," "He is going to hurt me again" and "I am dirty because of what he did to me." As she embraced each of these lies, the Holy Spirit revealed the following truths: "You are innocent; it was not your fault. You are safe now. You are not dirty because of what he did; rather, he defiled himself." When she heard these words, the perfect peace of Christ permeated her mind and heart. I asked her if any negative emotions remained in the memory. She reflected for a moment and then reported, "All I feel is release and peace, with a little sense of sadness."

I assumed that she was referring to the sorrow and grief she felt for herself for having gone through such an atrocity, and replied, "It is normal to feel this way about yourself for this loss you experienced."

Surprised, she said, "Oh no, I do not feel this for myself. I am okay. I feel fine. I can look at that memory and all I feel is peace and release from all the bad feelings. I just really feel sorry for that man. He must have been very lonely and hurting to have come to the place to do what he did to me."

This woman felt true compassion and forgiveness. I never led her through any prayer of forgiveness. I did not have to point her to my favorite Scripture passages on forgiveness. I did not have her accept her bad feelings after the prayer by faith, or reckon anything to be so. She was free, just like the king who "felt compassion and released him [the servant] and forgave him the debt" (Matt. 18:27). Forgiveness and compassion are natural by-products that result when lies are replaced with truth.

Sometimes a person finds complete peace in the memory, receives biblically consistent truth and yet cannot find the compassion from which to forgive the person who has hurt him or her. This doesn't necessarily indicate that renewal has not occurred in the memory. More likely, the person's inability to find compassion is due to other lies still present in other memories or something still needing to be exposed in the current memory. We must discover the specific reasons for our anger, rage, resentment and lack of forgiveness.

Too often people are led or manipulated to pray blanket prayers for all of their anger or inability to forgive. Yet how can we forgive if we do not know why we need to do so? In Matthew 18 it says the king took an account of what the servant owed him before he forgave him. We are *specifically* hurt, angry and resentful, and it is in these specific places that we must find release. We are angry for specific reasons in specific places. If we are going to find true release, we must visit those specific places and receive truth from the Holy Spirit *in each one.* Once we receive His truth and find perfect peace, we will also experience genuine compassion for those who have hurt us—even our abusers.

Much of what we have been taught about forgiveness is really nothing more than suppression of our pain. It doesn't usually work to simply just choose to forgive and let it go. This is suppression and denial of the pain within. Genuine forgiveness is possible only as we find release from the emotional pain held rooted in our lie-based thinking. When we find His peace we can then experience compassion and truly let it go.

Is There Evidence of Life Transformation as a Result of the Mind Renewal?

I am sure it was incredible for the blind man to receive his sight the day Jesus touched his eyes, but even more remarkable was the way his life surely changed from that moment forward. After his renewal he would not be found down by the city gates, begging; now he could go down to the local employment office and apply for a job. Those who receive renewal from their emotional memories no longer have to live in their crippled state. When the blind man received his sight, he did not have to work at seeing. When the emotionally crippled receive their "legs" back, they do not have to practice feeling peaceful and calm in those areas of their thinking. They will feel what the truth says. We feel what we believe.

True recovery means that we are free from the old pain and lies. True recovery is deep inner renewal that transforms naturally, without effort, into our daily walks and behavior. Once the lies are removed from our experiential knowledge and we find perfect peace, we are in a place where we can appropriate the Word of God in our lives.

For me, transformation is the primary test of whether I have received genuine renewal or not. If the same places that used to be guaranteed emotional landmines no longer trigger me or stir me, I rejoice in the peace of Christ. There are unmistakably places in my marriage that used to always be troublesome that are no longer a bother and require no effort to maintain. I know that because of this transformation, I have been truly released in many places where I was in bondage before.

Additional Evidence of Mind Renewal

As I have personally witnessed hundreds of people and received thousands of reports from others who find hope and release from their lifelong pain and struggle, I have observed the following.

True Renewal Is Permanent

I used to fear whether this dynamic change in people's lives could really last. If so, how long would it last? Would it fade away with time, like a posthypnotic suggestion? Would they have a relapse? When I first began to use Theophostic Prayer Ministry I had a secret fear that everyone who had received renewal would one day come back in worse shape than when they had first come for ministry. This fear has proved unfounded.

Sometimes people will come back after renewal and report that they are having more bad feelings. They sometimes assume that they are regressing or that they didn't receive renewal. Yet in every case thus far, the "return" of the old feelings has meant that the memory contained additional lies that were missed or had not yet surfaced or new places of pain had become stirred needing renewal. As these additional places received ministry, the same peace followed in these areas as well.

True Renewal Impacts Present Relationships

People often come to counseling because of the problems they are having with other people. They think, *If I am upset then you must be my problem, since you are in the room when I feel badly.*

Remember, however, our present conflict is rarely the source of our emotional pain. If a person is willing to put the present situation on hold in order to receive renewal for the historical wounds in his or her life, that person can find peace and release in the midst of the current problem. When this happens, that person's perspective of the present can change. What was troublesome before often becomes more manageable, and sometimes entirely free and clear. The issues that kept the person stirred up and dominated his or her current life vanish along with the historical lies.

You can be free and walk in peace, whether people around you change or not. You may be surprised at how many people stop doing what they do when you are no longer stirred up by it.

Now and then one of my twin daughters comes to me upset because of what her older brother is doing to her. I sometimes say, "The only reason he does what he does is because he knows it gets a rise out of you." The same is true in our adult relationships. I do what I do because you respond the way you do, and then I respond to your response. I trigger your pain, and your painful response triggers my pain. Change in either one of us can stop the cycle.

I remember one night, before I had the opportunity to access some of my lies and gain the measure of freedom I now know, Sharon asked me a question about my work. I felt attacked by her question, though now I realize there was nothing malicious in her statement. Still, I responded from my pain and she responded from her wound. We cycled our individual woundedness back and forth until we both were thoroughly exasperated.

However, since Sharon and I have been freed in this area through Theophostic Prayer Ministry, this particular cycle no longer emerges. Where there is no trigger, there is no pain, and when there is no pain there is no conflict. If you have to work at having a happy marital relationship, your effort is a good indication that you have wounded memories containing lies that need to be expelled and replaced with truth. When we were dating, Sharon and I didn't trigger each other's lies too much, and our relationship was easy. Once married the lies surfaced and we had to start working at loving each other. Now that the lies are being replaced with truth, we can share genuine love for each other with little effort. We both are choosing daily to go to our places of pain and to find truth. Every place we find truth and experience God's peace, we no longer have any conflict with each other. If we cannot trigger each other, we do not have conflict. We do have differences of opinion, but these situations can be approached without the pain of the past.

True Renewal Is Maintenance-Free

As we have already discussed, tolerable recovery usually requires an ongoing effort to maintain, and relapse threatens constantly. Yet true renewal is accomplished through what God does, not through our own efforts. If we do not do anything to affect a change, we cannot do anything to maintain it either. Renewal is much like salvation of our spirit. It is "by grace are ye saved through faith . . . not of works [self-effort], lest any man should boast" (Eph. 2:8-9, *KJV*).

I used to ignorantly misinform survivors of sexual abuse and other traumas that they would have to learn to compensate for the emotional damage they had received from their abuse, since they could never know complete renewal. I tried to instill a sense of hope by telling them a story of a man who had lost his legs in an auto accident, who, while he would never walk again, could live a productive life as he learned to compensate in other ways for his losses. I led them to believe they would get better, but that they would have to learn to live with the permanent damage done by the abuse. I no longer believe this.

Real renewal does not require compensation. If I am recovered, then I am recovered. If I am healed, I can take up my bed and walk, not crawl or limp around in compensation. I often see people who were emotionally lame take up their beds and walk when God reveals His truth in their lie-filled memories.

Remember that abstinence is rooted in self-control and self-effort, but healing and renewal are acts of God. Abstinence is a constant battle maintained by self-control.

If I am struggling not to do something, then I am not experiencing victory.

God didn't ever expect us to keep the law. The law exposed and condemned each of us because by it no one could ever be justified.

For as many as are of the works of the Law are under a curse; for it is written, "Cursed is everyone who does not abide by all things written in the book of the Law, to perform them." Now that no one is justified by the Law before God is evident . . . Christ redeemed us from the curse of the Law, having become a curse for us—for it is written, "Cursed is everyone who hangs on a tree"—in order that in Christ Jesus the blessing of Abraham might come to the Gentiles, so that we might receive the promise of the Spirit through faith (Gal. 3:10-11, 13-14).

Since we are no longer under the Law, sin has no power over us. However, when our pain is stirred, we will look for a means of dealing with what is stirred up, which often means sinful choices and behavior. Even though experiential truth from God is our only way of escape, most people look in other places to resolve it. Some look to pleasure, addictions, work and relationships, while others seek to deflect it through blaming others, life situations and even God.

We need to renew our minds so that we are not drawn aside by the lust of the flesh, which wages war with our minds (see Rom. 7:23).

As we are renewed in our minds we will be filled with the knowledge of His will in all spiritual wisdom and understanding, freeing us to walk in a manner worthy of the Lord, to please Him in all respects, resulting in the bearing fruit in every good work and increasing in the knowledge of God; strengthened with all power, according to His glorious might, for the attaining of all steadfastness and patience; joyously giving thanks to the Father, who has qualified us to share in the inheritance of the saints in Light (see Col. 1:9-13).

You really can know the "peace of God, which passes all comprehension" (Phil. 4:7), walk in genuine victory and release those who have hurt you. I say this because I have found peace in places that I had never known peace before as I have allowed the Spirit of Christ to lead me into places that I did not want to go in my memories and have felt the pain those memories contained. I have found peace in every memory that I have visited, and look forward to the freedom that is still yet to come.

In summary, genuine renewal will exhibit characteristics that demonstrate its validity. The renewal will be permanent and will require no maintenance to sustain it. It will result in lifestyle changes and enhanced personal relationships. The final outcome will be the presence of true compassion and forgiveness of those who have hurt us. Forgiveness is not something we have to work at, but rather is a natural by-product of genuine renewal and resultant compassion. If we can't forgive, it's merely evidence that there are still areas of lie-based thinking from which we need to find freedom.

In the next chapter we'll discuss the basic principles of genuine forgiveness as experienced in the context of Theophostic Prayer Ministry.

Chapter Six

Releasing Those Who Have Hurt Us

How Many Times Must I Forgive Someone?

In Matthew 18 Jesus teaches Peter and the other disciples about genuine forgiveness in response to Peter's question, How many times do I need to forgive? Seven times? (see v. 21). Jesus tells him, "I tell you, not seven times, but seventy-seven times" (v. 22). I can almost see Peter's shoulders slump at this point. I suspect that Peter asked Jesus this because he had forgiven someone many times, yet the person was not changing his behavior, and Peter was tired and hoping there was a forgiveness quota.

Jesus goes on to tell this story:

For this reason the kingdom of heaven may be compared to a certain king who wished to settle accounts with his slaves. And when he had begun to settle them, there was brought to him one who owed him ten thousand talents [about millions in current United States dollars]. But since he did not have the means to repay [remember, he was a servant on slave wages], his lord commanded him to be sold, along with his wife and children and all that he had, and repayment to be made. The slave therefore falling down, prostrated himself before him, saying, "Have patience with me, and I will repay you everything" [which was a lie, since he had no money]. And the lord of that slave felt compassion and released him and forgave him the debt. But that slave went out and found one of his fellow slaves who owed him a hundred denarii [about a day's wage]; and he seized him and began to choke him, saying, "Pay back what you owe." So his fellow slave fell down and began to entreat him, saying, "Have patience with me and I will repay you." He was unwilling however, but went and threw him in prison until he should pay back what was owed (Matt. 18:23-30).

The traditional interpretation of this passage is that Jesus is trying to teach His disciples about the great love God has for us and the forgiveness He offers all who come to Him to receive it. I believe this passage also teaches us some important truths about forgiveness and how we can find release from those who have hurt us.

Take an Account

Principle One: *Forgiveness requires we take an account.* "And when he had begun to settle them [the accounts of the servants], there was brought to him one who owed him ten thousand talents" (Matt. 18:24).

The king called his servants to give an account of what was owed because we cannot forgive a debt we do not know exists or if we do not know what the amount is on the note (here again is an example of dealing with the specific reasons for offense). Theophostic Prayer Ministry helps you to identify the specific reason for your pain by helping you follow the painful emotional trail back to the source of your emotional pain. Until you know what was done to you and the extent of the damage, you cannot completely forgive the offender.

People dissociate and bury their emotional pain in order to avoid feeling it all the time, but the pain has to be exposed before the true debt can be realized. All of us suppress bad feelings at times. This was one of my primary defenses against emotional pain as a child and for most of my adult life. If I felt bad about something I would just push the bad feelings down. By pushing the feelings down I was also suppressing the memory picture of the event itself. If you do this long enough, you will forget that the event even happened. The mind simply relocates the memory outside of your conscious reality.

Yet if we want true freedom from our offender, we must access the memory of the offenses, so we can take an account of them.

A Debt Only Jesus Can Repay

Principle Two: If we look to the offender for renewal, restitution or compensation we will only be more wounded. The one who has caused the pain does not have the means to repay the debt or remove the pain from our lives. "He did not have the means to repay" (Matt. 18:25).

The servant had a wife and children and was living on slave wages or less. He did not have the means to repay the millions he owed the king. The king needed to know what the servant owed, but he also realized that the servant couldn't repay this enormous debt—in several lifetimes.

Often wounded people will look to their abuser for repayment. For example, when Tim came to me for ministry, he was a depressed and frustrated businessman. He described himself as a workaholic and very driven. I asked him to tell me about his relationship with his father, as there is often a correlation between emotionally driven men and their "Daddy wounds."

Many times a man's driven, workaholic behavior is the vain attempt of a suppressed little boy still looking to his father for approval and acceptance. The father's emotional absence in the boy's life created an insatiable wound that has never been filled. When the man was a little boy, he had a God-created need to receive love, acceptance and approval from his father. This need went unmet, and the result was a wound that neither the wounder nor anyone else could ever fill. The same is true for those who marry looking for someone to meet their childhood needs that have become wounds. No one can address these wounds and take away the pain. The only remedy is God's renewal.

Tim went on to describe a father who was distant and often gone. To that day Tim's father still would not respond with words of affirmation when Tim would call and report his business successes. At one moment in our conversation Tim said, "No matter what I do, he never notices!" and began to weep. Tim was looking to one who did not have the means to repay for collection. This will never work.

Survivors of horrendous abuse as reported by people who claim to have ritual abuse memories (SRA), often feel a huge emotional void and live in a constant cycle of defeat because the void can never be filled.[1] Compassionate Christian ministers who try to fill these insatiable "love voids" may burn out trying to fill them. The truth is, only Jesus can heal this wound. The debt is too great, and only He can pay it back and restore the losses of these lives. God promises: "And I will restore to you the years that the locust hath eaten, the cankerworm, and the caterpillar, and the palmerworm, my great army which I sent among you. And ye shall eat in plenty, and be satisfied, and praise the name of the Lord your God, that hath dealt wondrously with you: and my people shall never be ashamed" (Joel 2:25-26, KJV).

When we seek to find resolution or restitution from those who were responsible for our original wounding or look to others later in life to fill these vacuums we will always be disappointed. Only truth from the Holy Spirit, spoken softly and gently, can calm the raging waves of our painful past.

Anger Must Be Released

Principle Three: *Anger is a normal reaction to injustice but must be released before freedom will come.* "But since he did not have the means to repay, his lord commanded him to be sold, along with his wife and children and all that he had, and repayment to be made" (Matt. 18:25).

When the king came to realize the severity of the situation, it appears that he reacted with anger. It looks like he may have even overreacted a bit. Not only did he command the servant to be sold into slavery, he sent the wife and innocent children away with him. It appears that the king was good and stirred up, and rightfully so. The king's anger was actually a normal and healthy response to this servant's apparent irresponsible behavior. How this servant could have ever gotten so deeply in debt is difficult to comprehend. The king knew the money was gone and he was never going to get it back. All there was to do was become angry and rightly punish the servant.

The Christian community has little tolerance for anger as an emotion. We're told that anger is sin and that true spiritual people don't get angry. Many parents also teach their children not to express their anger. Yet the Bible tells us to "be angry, and yet do not sin" (Eph. 4:26). Sinless anger sounds like an oxymoron. Anger becomes a sin when it is harbored and festers, or if it is acted out unrighteously. Paul describes how sinful anger originates in the last part of this verse when he says, "Don't let the sun go down on your anger or you will give the devil an opportunity."

Satan wants us to dwell on our anger day after day and do nothing about it. He wants us to turn the anger inward and bury it deeply. The reason for this is so that later, when something else happens that is remotely similar to the original offense, the demonic forces will take the opportunity to stir up this old anger so that we will react inappropriately and express more anger than the situation calls for. The problem with expressing old anger in a new situation is it never depletes the original anger. Until the anger is identified and then released by surrendering it to the Lord Jesus in the context of the original event (memory), we are destined to perpetually dump the old anger on whoever happens to trigger the original memory. It is not that we are just angry people. We are specifically angry in specific places for legitimate reasons. However, new events trigger this legitimate anger and it is illegitimately released in the new context. It is here that Satan has been given opportunity (see Eph. 4:26).

Forgiveness Is Not Dependent on the Offender

Principle Four: *The integrity and sincerity of the indebted wounder is not critical for true forgiveness to be administered.* "The slave therefore falling down, prostrated himself before him, saying, 'Have patience with me, and I will repay you everything'" (Matt. 18:26).

At first glance it seems the servant has come to his senses and is truly sorry for what he has done. However, something the servant says reveals his true heart even in that moment. When he promised, "I will repay you everything," he lied and revealed a heart of deceit. He knew that he could never repay his debt, and he had no intention of ever doing so. The fact that he had run up such an enormous debt tells us that he was a thief through irresponsible behavior.

Many times we want to offer forgiveness that's contingent on the attitude and integrity of the one we are forgiving. Yet genuine forgiveness has nothing to do with the condition of the one being forgiven. Forgiveness is not dependent on the person wanting or asking for it. Forgiveness is *aphiemy*, a cutting off, a release or sending away of the offense or debt. The king can cut off the debt, whether the servant wants it or has a change of heart or not.

Forgiveness is focused on the debt, not the debtor. When John the apostle wrote, "If we confess our sins, He is faithful and just to *forgive us our sins* and to cleanse us from all unrighteousness" (1 John 1:9, emphasis added), the focus of forgiveness is on the sin, not the sinner. The sin receives the action of the verb *forgive*. God releases or cuts off the sin, not the sinner. Actually, to pray correctly, we ought to say, "God forgive my sin," not "forgive me." I do not want God to cut me off, but I do want Him to release me of my sin and debt.

Forgiveness Requires Compassion

Principle Five: *Genuine forgiveness requires that we find compassion.* "And the lord of that slave felt compassion and released him and forgave him the debt" (Matt. 18:27).

If we try to forgive while we are still feeling the pain of the offense, forgiveness will be impossible. When we are able to follow our pain to its true source and find God's truth, the pain of the offense leaves. When the pain is gone, it will be replaced with peace and a sense of compassion. The peace and compassion we feel enable us to truly release another's debt.

The king felt compassion, and this allowed him freely to release the servant of the debt. His compassion for the servant exposed the true heart of the king and his true belief system. Compassion is the benevolent action we take toward another as a result of our own renewal, and the resulting emotional identification we are able to make with the one who has offended us. When we come into truth and receive God's grace and forgiveness, we can more clearly see the person who has hurt us from God's perspective. We are able to identify with the offender as a fellow sinner who is in need of truth, just as we are. I can forgive you when I see in you that which is also present in at least some measure in myself. I may not have ever sexually abused anyone, but I have offended others with my words and actions in other ways.

Apparently the Church of Rome had a non-compassionate, judging attitude toward others, which caused Paul to write "you are without excuse, every man of you who passes judgment, for in that you judge another, you condemn yourself; for you who judge practice the same things" (Rom. 2:1). These Roman Christians had not yet identified themselves in the lives of others. When we come into the truth God has for us and receive His perfect peace, we can experience the release of the need for revenge and the cutting off of the debt (forgiveness). When the king found compassion, he released the slave and forgave the debt.

Sharon and I had been married about 10 years when the Lord blessed us with our first child. Sarah was a delightful child who had an effervescent personality that could win over anyone's heart. However, this blessing came to a tragic end when little Sarah developed an undetected brain hemorrhage. She survived three brain surgeries, but eventually lost her fight for life and the Lord took her home. Sharon and I entered into the darkest time of our lives as we grieved the loss of our little girl.

Before Sarah died, I had already begun to counsel people who came to me with different issues and losses. Now and then someone would come who had suffered the loss of a loved one. I would say, "I know how you feel," and give other pat answers. The truth is, I did not know how they felt, because I had not experienced anything like what they were experiencing. I could offer sympathy but not compassion. Sympathy says, "I feel sorry for you." Compassion says, "I know the pain you carry, for I, too, have carried a similar burden."

Compassion can bear up the one in pain in a way that nothing else can. This is only possible because we can feel the pain. Many people tried to console me through my grief, and I appreciated it. However, when someone came and said, "I know what you feel; I, too, have experienced the death of a child," something inside of me reached out and grabbed hold of that person's words of encouragement. This person knew the pain of what I was feeling and could offer me true compassion.

The Scripture says that the king "felt compassion" (Matt. 18:27). I do not know what the king saw in the servant, because we know the servant wasn't sincere, but something struck the chords of compassion in the king's heart. The king "released him and forgave him his debt" (v. 27).

Forgiveness Offers Emotional Release

Principle Six: *Forgiveness emotionally releases the one offering the forgiveness, but may have no impact on the one whose debt is cleared.* The king "released him and forgave him the debt. But that slave went out and found one of his fellow slaves who owed him a hundred denarii [a day's wage]; and he seized him" (Matt. 18:27-28).

Notice the two contrasting words in this verse: released and seized. Here you see the true benefactor of forgiveness. When the king *released* the servant, he became free of the anger and the stresses of maintaining the note. The servant, on the other hand, was still in bondage to his evil heart, and *seized* his fellow worker.

Jesus wanted Peter to understand that forgiveness frees the forgiver. The fellow who caused trouble for Peter needed to be forgiven so that Peter could be free. Peter's concern was how long he would have to carry his resentment, frustration and pain before he could cut this guy off and bury him, as the king had planned to do to the servant. Jesus suggested here that if Peter looked closely enough at this man, he might just find something with which he could identify. He might discover, like the lady I mentioned earlier, that his offender, like her abuser, was a lonely, hurting soul who was also deceived and wounded by lies that needed God's grace and mercy.

When we forgive someone, it doesn't mean that person will change his or her offensive behavior. Only God can change people; and He will do so only if they want to change. Of course, our forgiveness could have a positive impact on the offender and might motivate that person to seek change and renewal, but we have no guarantee this will happen.

Forgiveness has the power to change only the one forgiving, not the one being forgiven. The good news is that we can be emotionally free from other people and their behavior, whether they ever change or not. Other people's behavior does not have the power to control us emotionally. Of course, people do exert control over others in marriages and other relationships, but this is not true control. The one being controlled believes the lie that the other person has control over him or her. If we believe that we are powerless and weak (even though we are not), we will be rendered powerless by others' words and actions.

Battered wives are dominated by their husband's emotional control, and that's why they feel trapped. Of course, in some cases the husband physically holds the wife against her will, but most of the time the woman cannot be free because she does not believe she can be. The angry husband triggers her childhood lie-based thinking, causing her to feel the same powerlessness that she may have felt as a child in a similar abusive situation. As a child, she was helpless and powerless to do anything to change her world, but today she is an adult. The problem is that her childhood experiential feelings are more powerful than the logical truth of the present.

If Peter forgave his offender 7 times 70 (490 times), he would still be in the same place as he started if he did not find freedom from the bondage he had with his offender. The number of times we forgive will have little or no impact on whether the person who has offended us will act differently in the future. When we forgive, we must do so without any expectation that the person being forgiven will change. We must let go of any expectation that the one who wounded us will or can repay the debt. Christ can release us from the pain of the wounder's indebtedness, as we are willing to let go and look to Him who can replace pain with perfect peace.

Forgiveness Is Not Reconciliation

Principle Seven: *Forgiveness should not be confused with reconciliation.* There is no indication that the king and the servant ever became friends, ate lunch together or sat with each other in church. As a matter of fact, the Scripture says their relationship never got any better than it was the day the servant was called in to give an account. Yet the king truly released the servant and forgave him his debt.

Remember, forgiveness is focused on the debt, not the debtor. My banker could call me and inform me that he has made the decision to cancel all my debts. It really does not matter if I am happy, grateful, desirous or even willing to receive. If he chooses to release me of the debt, I have no choice but to be released. I can scream, cuss or protest loudly. I can tell him I will not accept it. I can even continue to send in my monthly payments, but the bottom line is, I owe the bank nothing if the banker decides to tear up my note.

The power to forgive lies totally in the hands of the one who holds the note. The one in debt has nothing to say about whether forgiveness occurs. Reconciliation, however, is a completely different matter, and the two shouldn't be confused. Forgiveness is letting go of the debts others owe you. Reconciliation is about relationship. I cannot have a relationship with someone who has hurt me, yet has never come clean with what he or she has done. Relationship requires transparency and integrity from both parties. I can forgive you (release you of your debt) whether you want me to or not, but I cannot be reconciled to you until you accept responsibility for your sin. Reconciliation requires the debtor to take full responsibility for his or her actions, confess the error of his or her way and in penitent brokenness seek reconciliation from the one he or she has offended. At this time the one offended is in the position to receive God's grace to enter into relationship if he or she chooses.

However, if the debtor does not admit the wrong and accept full responsibility for his or her offense, reconciliation is not possible. Paul says, "If possible, *so far as it depends on you,* be at peace with all men" (Rom. 12:18, emphasis added). Reconciliation is based upon relationship. You cannot have relationship in the context where an offender refuses to do the right thing.

I used to believe recovery from abuse necessitated confronting one's abuser. I believed that as victims of abuse became more emotionally stable and strong, they would need to confront and hold their abusers accountable. Somehow I believed that doing this would empower them. I now see that this is not true or necessary. As people come into perfect peace, they are able to view their abusers through the eyes of Christ, with genuine compassion and forgiveness. It is here they find true freedom.

Sometimes the victim stills feels a need to confront, but it is done from a different posture than before. I used to encourage victims to connect with their righteous anger on the inside and use this as strength to face those who had hurt them. Today I neither encourage nor discourage confrontation. If the person feels a need to confront, I want to discern what is driving the need to do so. If it is anger, revenge or any other negative emotion, I encourage the person to continue in renewal until he or she can confront with perfect peace. When we confront from a place of peace rather than anger, the impact on the one accused of the abuse is incredible. There is much more power in confronting with peace than in doing so with anger.

The members of my sexual abuse survivors' group were some of the first recipients of Theophostic Prayer Ministry. Wanda was a young lady who had worked very hard for several years with me, and she was finally experiencing freedom as we used the Theophostic Prayer Ministry approach to renewal. Wanda had been abused by her grandfather many times as a little girl. Before she underwent Theophostic Prayer Ministry, the very thought of confronting him caused her to feel small and powerless. We practiced the confrontation many times in group sessions through role-playing and talking to empty chairs, but Wanda made very little progress in this area.

As we began to use Theophostic Prayer Ministry, she became less and less fearful, and the feelings of powerlessness vanished as her lies were replaced with truth. She said that it was as if she was growing up on the inside with each renewal moment. She reported feeling more and more like an adult, rather than feeling like a little child all the time. When she thought of the abusive memories, she felt strong and confident and had perfect peace.

Wanda called me at home one night a few days after finding release from her fears. She was very emotional when she first started speaking, and I thought she was having a crisis and needed help. It suddenly occurred to me, however, that she was excited, not upset. She told me, "Well, I did it!"

I had no idea what it was she had done, so I asked, "Did what?"

She went on to tell me that she had confronted her grandfather. Just by chance she had come face-to-face with him in the city park earlier that same day. When she saw him, she said she had expected to feel childlike, fearful and overwhelmed. Instead, she felt no fear or panic, only calmness and confidence. She walked over to him and proceeded to confront him with what he had done to her. She did not feel angry, small or fearful, and wasn't acting out of revenge. She was simply letting him know that the secret was out and that he was going to have to face it and its consequences.

After she finished telling him all she wanted to say, he denied it, but his response didn't bother her. She simply restated the facts with the same adultlike confidence. When he saw that she was not wavering, he began to panic and expressed fear of being put in jail and begged her not to tell anyone else. She told him that at this point she had forgiven him, and would leave the consequences of his crime to God and move on with her life. She also let him know that her forgiveness did not release him of being responsible for his actions in relation to God or those whom he had hurt.

Later on she did report his crimes to some members of the family she suspected he had also hurt. Several of her cousins came forward with similar stories of their grandfather's abuse.

The change in Wanda's feelings and behavior clearly indicates her genuine renewal and newfound freedom.

Again, I am not suggesting that victims confront their abusers. This is between the person and God. Yet when genuine renewal occurs, a change of perspective also occurs. Victims see their abusers through the eyes of Christ, and they can do the impossible by forgiving their abusers with genuine heartfelt compassion. Jesus truly loves the vilest of sinners and desires for their complete redemption. When victims receive His eyes, they are released to love with His love.

What Will You Do with Your Pain?

You may have people in your life with whom you are angry, bitter or resentful — and you probably have a right to feel this way. If they hurt you unjustly then they were wrong. Yet what are you going to do with this pain? You may believe that the anger protects you from further abuse or harm. This is not true. You may believe that if you forgive your abuser then he or she will be getting away with the crime. This also is not true. The anger, hate and desire for revenge onto which you hold are stealing the good things that God has for you. He will go with you to the painful places in your mind and remove the deep hurt. He is willing to relieve you of all the anger and resentment, if you will allow Him to do so.

If you are in emotional bondage to someone who has hurt you, I encourage you to seek ministry from someone who understands the principles in this book and to go to Jesus with your pain. "Cast all your anxieties on him, for he [really] cares about you" (1 Pet. 5:7, *RSV*).

Chapter Seven

Answers to Common Questions About Theophostic Prayer Ministry

People often ask me about Theophostic Prayer Ministry. This chapter addresses some of the more general questions people have about the basis of the ministry; it also seeks to dispel some of the misconceptions about Theophostic Prayer Ministry that have surfaced on the Internet.

Are the Theophostic Principles in the Bible?

Theophostic Prayer Ministry is found in the Bible right after the section that discusses heart surgery, magnetic resonance imaging (MRI) and brain surgery. It is interesting to watch people criticize TPM on this point yet do not think twice about utilizing medical science when they have a need for such. Theophostic Prayer Ministry is based both upon biblical and neurological principles. Since God created the mind and how it functions, God is the author of both. The two primary biblical principles of this ministry are the necessity of *prayer* and *encouragement* of each other.[1] We are biblically commanded to both pray for each other and to continually encourage each other in the faith. These two facets are foundational for genuine Theophostic Prayer Ministry. Theophostic Prayer Ministry is simply intercessory prayer to God for the ministry recipient coupled with encouragement. I, the facilitator, seek to pray and petition God on your behalf (intercession). I do this by asking the Lord what He desires for you to do (your willful choice) and what He wants you to know (truth and belief). During this prayerful context I will continually encourage you to feel what you need to feel, to seek to discern and figure out what may be hindering the process and to discover what it is you believe in the memory context that is causing you emotional duress. There are other biblical principles taught in Theophostic Prayer Ministry but these are non-essential for doing this ministry and primarily my opinions and interpretations.

Back to the original question of whether the Bible supports Theophostic Prayer Ministry. I suppose the first question to ask should be, Is the word *theophostic* in the Bible? The answer is no. That is, unless you break it down into its New Testament Greek root word form of *theos*, which means God, and *phos*, which means light.

Are the neurological principles of Theophostic Prayer Ministry listed or discussed in the Bible? No, the writers of the Bible did not have these concepts from which to draw any more than they did any other scientific or medical framework. The Early Church did not understand many concepts that are commonplace for us today and accepted as truth such as, the concept of blood pressure, infectious germs or antibiotics. In the same way, much of what we know concerning how the mind works is non-biblical information but nonetheless true. God designed and created the realities of the mind and much of the non-biblical yet scientifically true principles of Theophostic Prayer Ministry rely upon them. However, many of the basic principles of Theophostic Prayer Ministry can be found in subtle forms throughout the Bible. They are evident in the way God has dealt with people throughout history.

Theophostic Prayer Ministry is not a new concept. What God is doing through this ministry process is the same as He has done throughout the ages. He desires that we know the truth and walk in it. God uses daily situations, people and life in general to test us, and expose us so that He might renew our thinking. Theophostic Prayer Ministry is about intentionally moving people to the place where they can receive truth at an experiential level. Theophostic Prayer Ministry is a systematized format by which this is more easily accomplished.

The Bible is full of examples of how God has operated within the principles taught in this approach to ministry. For example, we can see them operating in Peter's life when viewed through all four Gospel accounts. The process is common for all. Peter finds himself being exposed (fear) by the Lord's words concerning the forthcoming crucifixion. Peter responds from his fear-based lies with arrogance and supposed confidence, "I will lay down my life for You" (John 13:37). His true belief system is exposed in the outer court where he denies the Lord three times. Later following the resurrection the Lord reveals truth to Peter, resulting in Peter's restoration and eventual transformation.

The setting was the night that Jesus was to be betrayed. The Lord was telling His disciples about His coming arrest and death.

Jesus said to them, "You will all become deserters because of me this night; for it is written, 'I will strike the shepherd, and the sheep of the flock will be scattered.' But after I am raised up, I will go ahead of you to Galilee." Peter said to him, "Though all become deserters because of you, I will never desert you." [This was not the truth and apparently driven by the fear that was stirred up in Peter that we later see manifested in his denial of Christ.] Jesus said to him, "Truly I tell you, this very night, before the cock crows, you will deny me three times." Peter said to him, "Even though I must die with you, I will not deny you" (Matt. 26:31-35, *NRSV*)

Jesus further said to Peter,

Simon, Simon, listen! Satan has demanded to sift all of you like wheat, but I have prayed for you that your own faith may not fail; and you, when once you have turned back, strengthen your brothers." And [Peter] said to him, "Lord, I am ready to go with you to prison and to death" (Luke 22:31-33, *NRSV*).

Jesus then led His disciples into the garden to pray. After He prayed, Judas came with a group of people to arrest Jesus. Then Simon Peter, who had a sword, drew it, struck the high priest's slave and cut off his right ear. The slave's name was Malchus. Jesus said to Peter, "Put the sword into the sheath; the cup which the Father has given me, shall I not drink it?" (John 18:11).

Then they seized him and led him away, bringing him into the high priest's house. But Peter was following at a distance. When they had kindled a fire in the middle of the courtyard and sat down together, Peter sat among them. Then a servant-girl, seeing him in the firelight, stared at him and said, "This man also was with him." But he denied it, saying, "Woman, I do not know him." A little later someone else, on seeing him, said, "You also are one of them." But Peter said, "Man, I am not!" Then about an hour later still another kept insisting, "Surely this man also was with him; for he is a Galilean." But Peter said, " Man, I do not know what you are talking about!" At that moment, while he was still speaking, the cock crowed. The Lord turned and looked at Peter. Then Peter remembered the word of the Lord, how he had said to him, "Before the cock crows today, you will deny me three times." And he went out and wept bitterly. (Luke 22:54-62, *NRSV*)

What followed was the Crucifixion, three days in the tomb and then the Resurrection. Many days after the Resurrection, Jesus appeared to His disciples early one morning while they were out fishing. He called to them and they came to land and had breakfast with Him. After they had eaten, a discussion arose between Jesus and Peter.

When they had finished breakfast, Jesus said to Simon Peter, "Simon son of John, do you love me more than these?" He said to him, "Yes, Lord; you know that I love you." Jesus said to him, "Feed my lambs." A second time he said to him, "Simon son of John, do you love me?" He said to him, "Yes, Lord; you know that I love you." Jesus said to him, "Tend my sheep." He said to him the third time, "Simon son of John, do you love me?" Peter felt hurt because he said to him the third time, "Do you love me?" And he said to him, "Lord, you know everything; you know that I love you." Jesus said to him, "Feed my sheep. Very truly, I tell you, when you were younger, you used to fasten your own belt and to go wherever you wished. But when you grow old, you will stretch out your hands, and someone else will fasten a belt around you and take you where you do not wish to go." (He said this to indicate the kind of death by which he would glorify God.) After this he said to him, "Follow me." Peter turned and saw the disciple whom Jesus loved following them; he was the one who had reclined next to Jesus at the supper and had said, "Lord, who is it that is going to betray you?" When Peter saw him, he said to Jesus, "Lord, what about him?" Jesus said to him, "If it is my will that he remain until I come, what is that to you? Follow me!" (John 21:15-22, *NRSV*).

This passage reveals some of the principles upon which Theophostic Prayer Ministry is based. The basic premises are: (1) We are all lie-based to some measure and need renewal of our minds, (2) God will either allow or orchestrate life so that what we believe is exposed, (3) when our false belief is exposed it will be made manifest through our emotional pain, (4) this emotional pain will have powerful influence on the choices we make, (5) if we choose to turn to Jesus He can renew our thinking with His truth and (6) transformation always follows an encounter with Christ.

First, Jesus exposed Peter's lie-based thinking. Jesus announced that He was about to be betrayed and killed, and that all the disciples would soon scatter. Peter boldly spoke out, saying that he would die before he would deny Jesus. Jesus exposed him on the spot when He said, "before the rooster crows today, you will deny three times that you know me" (Luke 22:34). Since we know that Peter would not be willing to die for Jesus, but instead would buckle in fear in just a few hours, we can safely say that Peter's proclamation was rooted in fear and not courage.

Peter's behavior is common to all of us. Something happens that triggers our lie-based thinking, which surfaces a negative emotion. Rather than coming clean with our feelings and our true thinking, we cover them over with a false presentation that puts us in a more positive light. Jesus' announcement of His forthcoming death triggered fear in Peter that he was unwilling to admit. Instead, Peter boasted of his commitment to die if necessary. Peter gave the right answer and the noble response (*logical truth*) but was not confessing his true feelings or his *experiential knowledge*. I believe Peter really wished that he could die if called to do so, and believed that this was the right thing to do, but his emotions did not match his logical data.

After Jesus prayed in the Garden of Gethsemane and the group came to arrest Him, Peter tried again to push through his fear when he cut off the man's ear. The Bible says that the disciples *all* fled as the soldiers arrested Jesus and led Him off to be tried.

Later we find Peter in the outer court while Jesus was being questioned. Here again Peter was trying his best to do the right thing. He was as close to the action as his fear would allow him. However, in the next few moments his fear was fully exposed. A woman at the gate questioned his connection to Jesus and Peter denied having been with Jesus. Then a little girl came up to him and identified him as one who had been with Jesus. This was as far as he could go with his performance-based spirituality, as he began to swear and angrily deny the Lord. The Scriptures say that as the rooster was crowing, Jesus looked over at him. The pain Peter must have felt when Jesus looked over at him in that moment must have surely been beyond comprehension.

Jesus was later crucified and placed in a tomb for three days, and then gloriously rose again. When He appeared to the disciples on the seashore it was to be His third appearance. I do not believe that Jesus did anything by chance. I believe that He intended to appear this third time to Peter in order to trigger the pain stored in Peter's mind concerning his denial of the Lord. It is also important to see how Jesus deliberately asked Peter three times if he loved Him. Even the Scriptures point this out when they say that it hurt Peter to hear the Lord ask Him the *third* time (see John 21:17). What was Jesus doing here? He was triggering and stirring up Peter's memory-based pain by way of association. Peter was now positioned to receive truth. It was in this moment of emotional pain that Jesus told Peter that he would indeed be willing to die for Him when he was old. Jesus said,

"Very truly, I tell you, when you were younger, you used to fasten your own belt and to go wherever you wished. But when you grow old, you will stretch out your hands, and someone else will fasten a belt around you and take you where you do not wish to go." [He said this to indicate the kind of death by which he would glorify God.] After this he said to him, "Follow me" (John 21:18-19, *NRSV*).

Peter wanted to be willing to die for Jesus and was deeply grieved that his fear had shut him down in the time of crisis. However, Jesus told him that there would come a time when he would pass the test and would lay down his life.

Prior to the denial of Christ, Peter spoke the correct answer when he proclaimed that he would die for Jesus. That was a good and right answer but it was just not what he really believed experientially in that moment. It appears that he was actually frightened and did not know what else to say. Satan indeed sifted him as wheat (exposed his lies), just as Jesus said he would, and Peter came up lacking when Satan exposed his true belief system, which was based on fear. He acted on this fear and denied the Lord three times.

I believe that when Peter heard the prophetic truth of his own death, the fear that had led to his denial of the Lord was erased from his mind. In the first few chapters of Acts we find Peter standing in front of an enormous crowd in the same city in which he denied Jesus and proclaiming Christ as His Messiah, and over 3,000 people were saved on that day.

The Bible is full of stories just like this. God has not changed His methods. He still allows us to be exposed, to fall apart emotionally and to make poor choices so that we will be motivated to seek Him in order to know truth. Jesus is still willing to speak to us in our pain and to provide His peace, if we will listen.

Theophostic Prayer Ministry is an intentional decision to be exposed of God in what we believe. It is the purposeful intent to feel the pain we typically run from, deny or deflect and follow it to its lie-based source. It is willfully working in harmony with what God is doing in us by intentionally submitting to the process when we are exposed in our pain.

Does Ed Smith Believe That He Has Received a Divine Revelation from God with this Process He Has Called Theophostic Prayer Ministry?

For the record, I do not believe that I have received any revelatory information from God, nor have I ever made such a claim.[2] As I discussed in the last question, I do not believe that Theophostic Prayer Ministry in concept is anything new just systematized and intentional. I regret the wording I used in an earlier edition of the Basic Training Seminar manual that was misinterpreted by an individual that apparently lead him to make this false claim of me. The truth is, tens of thousands of people read the same information and did not interpret me in this manner.

What I truly believe is that we do not need new revelation. I believe that the Scripture is complete and all we need. I believe that "all Scripture is given by inspiration of God, and is profitable for doctrine, for reproof, for correction, for instruction in righteousness, that the man of God may be complete, thoroughly equipped for every good work" (2 Tim. 3:16-17, *NKJV*). Insight I have had, special revelation as did the apostles, of course not. There is a big difference between having insight into the Scriptures (as all Bible students should have from time to time) and new revelation. Be aware as you go to the Internet and read where others are making the claim that I believe otherwise and know that these same people are clearly aware of my present clarification and yet they continue to propagate this falsehood anyway. This may raise question as to real their purpose and agenda.

Does Theophostic Prayer Ministry Teach That God Is Speaking New Revelation to People During Their Sessions That Supersedes or Is Equal in Status to the Scriptures?

Not at all. Again, when people report hearing, receiving or seeing some truth in their memory, they are *not* receiving new revelation. The Holy Spirit is giving them specific applications of established biblical truth for their memory situation. This is really no different than when someone says, "I was at work today and sensed the Lord wanted me to talk to my associate about his need for Christ." Did that person hear a word from God? I believe so. Was it extrabiblical? No, Scripture tells us, "Go therefore and make disciples" (Matt. 28:19). What is received in a ministry session will never contradict, replace or supersede the Word of God. If it does, then it is a falsehood and does not meet the test of Theophostic Prayer Ministry.

Theophostic Prayer Ministry is not a way to get an inside word from God. I once heard of a group of people who unwisely gathered together around a woman who was suffering from a dissociative disorder. They believed she had a direct line to God during her ministry sessions. They would have her ask God for direction for their own personal issues and lives. She would then channel the message from "God" back to them. She would also prophesy special words and messages from "God." *This is not Theophostic Prayer Ministry!* This looks much like divination and witchcraft. Stay clear of all forms of this practice.

Does Theophostic Prayer Ministry Use Guided Imagery, Directed Visualization or Some Form of Hypnosis?

A few misinformed people on the Internet have made this claim, which is false. These people have never contacted this ministry to get the facts, and instead they have interpreted the printed materials from their own preconceived notions. For the record, *Theophostic Prayer Ministry unequivocally denounces all forms of guided imagery, minister or counselor directed visualization and hypnosis.* Please visit our Web site and read the article comparing Theophostic Prayer Ministry with Recovered Memory Therapy for a more extensive discussion of this matter.

Some people report having visual images during the ministry session, and it is without question that visual pictures do play a part in a Theophostic session for *some* people. However, I believe that truth that comes in the form of mental pictures is simply one way that the Holy Spirit has chosen to reveal His truth to certain people. However, these pictures should never be the creation of the one administering the process. Anything in the mind of the person receiving ministry that is created by the minister is not Theophostic Prayer Ministry but rather visualization or guided imagery created by the minister or counselor.

I do acknowledge that in the early printed publications that this ministry produced were in transition and some of what I said seemed ambiguous. I regret this but I have been learning as I have grown in knowledge, experience and practice. Today the training materials are more clear and precise. See the Theophostic Prayer Ministry Guidelines for a summarization of what a Theophostic Prayer Ministry Session should look like.

Is There Any Danger That the One Administering Theophostic Prayer Ministry Might Implant False Information in a Person's Mind During a Ministry Session?

Theophostic Prayer Ministry is, in its most basic form, simply prayer. In this prayerful state people are encouraged to follow the painful emotions that are surfaced to their original place in memory. Theophostic Prayer Ministry works only with memories that the people being ministered to remember on their own, without the help, suggestions or insinuations of the one doing ministry. The minister should never suggest anything concerning the content of the person's memory during the process, no matter how convinced he or she may be of its validity. Theophostic Prayer Ministry teaches the minister to get out of the way and refrain from all forms of suggestion or insinuation. The minister should ask only questions that reflect the information that the person has already revealed. A minister should *never* say things like, "I wonder if someone molested you?" or "You have symptoms of being molested as a child," or "I think you may be SRA, or a survivor of a government mind control project." Such statements are completely misleading, are forbidden, are out of line and do not represent Theophostic Prayer Ministry in any form.

Theophostic Prayer Ministry does not lead a person to get into a relaxed or trance state any more so than any other typical ministry or counseling session. The person simply sits in a chair while reflecting on his or her present negative feelings. Theophostic Prayer

Ministry avoids the use of hypnotic practices in any form. The minister does not have the person count backward, think of a safe place or follow a swinging pocket watch. The minister simply asks the person to discern what he or she feels and why and pray.

When the person identifies an emotion, the minister encourages the person to look to see if there is a memory that contains the same or similar feelings. Some have accused Theophostic Prayer Ministry of implanting information because at times forgotten memories do surface in a session. The people making these accusations do not believe that a person can forget a traumatic event, yet a long history of research has clearly demonstrated that memories can be consciously denied for many different reasons. Many children who are abused deny the event as a way of surviving the abuse, and later may have no conscious awareness of the abuse, even as an adult. Evidence for repressed memory comes in many forms such as but not limited to: testimony from other eyewitnesses, confession from the perpetrator admitting the crime or previous medical documentation that supports the memory and matching scar evidence.

All of us have aspects of our lives held in memories we cannot consciously access. Who remembers every aspect of his or her life? How many of us have had memories from the distant past suddenly surface after being triggered during a present situation? Not too long ago something happened with me and immediately a memory surfaced that I did not recall ever having remembered since the event occurred originally. It was not until the current situation triggered the original event that I remembered it. However, when it surfaced I recalled the event in clear detail. We remember parts and places, but only selected events are actually consciously available at any given time. I used to inaccurately believe the mind was a video recorder capturing every part of our life in detail. Research is teaching us that memory is much more complex and requires careful handling to arrive at any conclusive understanding. Theophostic Prayer Ministry now stresses the importance of handling memories carefully and not coming to any fast conclusions. Theophostic Prayer Ministry is primarily focused on the false interpretations the recipient of ministry reports, stored in the memory context and not on validating everything that is reported.

Most of us experience moments of amnesia where we are not able to recall memory information from time to time. How frustrating it is when we run into someone and we cannot recall his name even though we know the information is in there somewhere. I am notorious for losing things. I lose my keys, my glasses and sometimes my car in the parking lot. As a matter of fact, as I write this paragraph I have lost a part of this computer (an extra hard drive) that I need but have no idea (consciously) where I have placed it. Yet the truth is, the hard drive is not really lost; my mind contains the information I need to find it. I just cannot access this information. As soon as I find the lost item, however, I will respond with something like, "Oh, yeah, that's where I left it." When I find the item, I will remember having placed it in that spot in the first place. It would be really nice if I could just command this information to surface, but I cannot. It has been stored outside of my conscious awareness.

In the same way, if something happens to me as a child that I do not want to remember, my mind can place the undesirable information in a place where I cannot consciously find it. This is a survival tactic. When my subconscious mind believes it is safe to release the information (as in a Theophostic session) it very well may release the painful memory.

Here again let me encourage you to read through the Theophostic Prayer Ministry Guidelines listed toward the end of this book to gain a quick summary of what a Theophostic Prayer Ministry session should look like.

How Do We Know That What People Are Reporting Are True Memories?

I minister to people who are in obvious pain. When they come to me for ministry, they have many symptoms that clearly indicate something is wrong. They do not come reporting that life is great, that they are happy and that all is well. I see people who are depressed, discouraged, self-loathing, angry, bitter, compulsive, self-mutilating, addicted and sometimes dissociated. Along with all manner of emotional pain, they often exhibit a variety of physical conditions that match their emotional maladies. I believe that these people have become this way as either a consequence of sinful choices or as a response to what has happened to them in life and because of their interpretation about what happened. I also acknowledge that some people are emotionally distressed due to physiological causes that are not lie-based. Theophostic Prayer Ministry is a self-discovery process seeking to uncover the true source of our emotional pain. In this process people sometimes end up in memories of which they were consciously unaware. Repression had afforded them the ability to function without having to consciously live in the trauma reality.

Theophostic Prayer Ministry assumes that the memory is a compilation of impressions, interpretations and recollections in the person's mind and not a perfect science. It's critical to discern what experiential belief is producing the emotional pain in the person's life. Discerning the accuracies of all the details in a memory, though important, is not the purpose or scope of Theophostic Prayer Ministry. Nevertheless, this aspect of memory work is something that must be attended to, especially where accusations are being made of others.

It is possible that a person might believe something happened that didn't, or that happened differently than the memory portrays it. For example, a man might surface a memory of being abandoned by his mother and left with relatives to be raised. He may believe his mother left him because she hated him and didn't want him, yet in reality the mother's heart may have broken when she had to let her child go due to forces beyond her ability to control. However, this is beside the point when it comes to the man's renewal. If he believes the lie that he was not wanted, then this wound needs to be healed. What we remember is our reality, and it is in this reality that renewal must occur.

Furthermore, a memory isn't invalidated simply because I do not have all the facts. I may not have all the data in the correct order, or all the dates lined up perfectly, for if I was hurt then I was hurt. If we can get all the facts straight this is good, but it is not essential for discerning the lies one believes and finding truth.

Can suggestible people make their way into a counselor's office and passively open up their minds while the counselor plants thoughts into them, creating false memories? Perhaps, although I think this must be very rare. To assume this is common is to discredit all the good ministers and counselors in our country who work with people who surface painful repressed events and to invalidate the hundreds of thousands of people reporting trauma. I believe it is possible for a person to be led to believe something occurred that in fact did not. However, I find it hard to fathom that people could believe a story to the extent that they would abreact in extreme emotional pain and lose their ability to function in daily life, develop mental disorders, be emotionally incapacitated and thus live in misery. Logic and rational thinking says that real pain has real-life sources. A false memory is just that—it is false. A false memory cannot produce traumatic pain to the extent of the above results. If people bear symptoms as listed here then there is a reason and labeling it all as chemical imbalance is unlikely.

The number of people who are reported to have had traumatic memory and then reneged and claimed false memory is miniscule compared to the enormous number of people who have reported trauma that has surfaced in ministry sessions and who believe their trauma to be true. If a person is making up a story for whatever reason, then the person hasn't had a false memory—the story isn't a memory. If a person has a memory that contains inaccurate information, this does not make the memory false; it simply means it's a memory with inaccurate information.

While it's important to discover the truth of what happened at some point, the lies producing the pain in the memory should be addressed first. I work in the reality of the people with whom I am ministering. To project my reality or my belief about their realities will have little effect in releasing them from their pain and in a sense I would be implanting potential falsehood. This is especially true as I work with victims of extreme abuse and trauma. Though these people have suffered the most horrible atrocities imaginable, God is still granting them truth and peace. Do I believe every detail of their experiences? No. Do I try to talk them out of their beliefs about such experiences? Never. I simply work in their reality and invite Christ to reveal His truth. Is it possible that not everything they report is true? Absolutely. Do I seek to help them discern the difference? When I am able.

Memory is not a pure science, but the lies found in people's memories can for the most part be discerned with clarity. Does this uncertainty invalidate people's reports of being abused or traumatized? Not at all. Generally I have no problem believing the essence of the stories that I hear. I acknowledge that every detail may not be totally accurate. When someone comes to me with traumatic emotional pain, something traumatic is likely the source. I assume that something occurred in the context of real-life experience. I do not assume that the person will have a perfect recollection of what occurred, but I hope to find enough evidence to establish what is believed in this experiential context. I look for the source of the pain (which of course is not the memory itself but the false interpretation in the memory).

What convinces me more than anything else of the reality of repressed memory is the people I see whose lives have been transformed through renewal in the context of these same memories. These souls have been in pain all their lives, suffered all manner of dysfunction and disorder, attempted to manage this pain with self-destructive behaviors but then finally come into *the perfect peace of Christ.* Many have done everything else available to alleviate their pain through traditional counseling, but only when they embrace their repressed memories and receive a freeing truth from God do they find peace.

The bottom line is, memory is stored experience. I might be able to create a false picture in a client's mind, but I cannot create a debilitating emotion arising from this false picture. Real pain is not a figment of one's imagination. Real pain has a real source. I might be able to convince little Johnny that he saw Superman at the theme park when in reality he actually saw Spiderman. In this case I have implanted false information in a true memory experience. This does not invalidate the fact that he went to the park and did see an action hero figure. However, I might have a more difficult time convincing little Johnny that he was sexually molested by Superman, if the molestation never occurred in the first place. It's a major leap from implanting the identity of an action hero figure to being sexually abused by one.

Does Jesus Actually Appear to People in Their Memories?

I do not think that Jesus Himself is physically appearing to people in their memories. The Scripture says, "[Jesus] alone possesses immortality and dwells in unapproachable light; whom no man has seen or can see" (1 Tim. 6:16). The next time anyone will truly see Jesus is when He returns in the clouds. Furthermore, people doing genuine Theophostic Prayer Ministry do not ask questions such as "Do you see Jesus?" or make suggestions such as "Look for Jesus." These kinds of directives would be guiding and creating imagery. This is *not* Theophostic Prayer Ministry.

However, I think it's possible that people can see a visual representation of Jesus in their memories. I would call this visual a word picture or visual communication between the person and God. I have seen hundreds of people come into perfect peace after encountering truth in a visual form during a Theophostic session.

Is Theophostic Prayer Ministry New Age or Any Other Secular Form of Helping People?

Theophostic Prayer Ministry is not based on any New Age concept or belief. It is totally Christ centered and Holy Spirit directed. Theophostic Prayer Ministry rests on the biblical principles of God's Word and on a basic understanding of what is known scientifically about how the mind works.

I do not endorse everything that is coming down the science pike, but there is an enormous amount of information available that has proven invaluable in increasing our effectiveness in mind renewal and ministry. God has given us minds to develop, and I believe that using the results of good research is being a good steward of what God has given us. Theophostic Prayer Ministry is being successfully used by thousands of churches and ministries all around the world who have found it to be biblically consistent and Jesus centered.

Does Theophostic Prayer Ministry Replace the Need for Biblical Instruction?

Not at all! In order to move toward maturity and completeness, every Christian needs discipleship, teaching, preaching and instruction. Yet I believe we have become somewhat unbalanced. We have, for the most part, become a cognitive Church, seeking to know God with our minds but not with our experience. I don't believe, as some do, that if our relationship with God is hindered that it is *always* because of sinful behavior or because we still have sinful hearts. Believers often struggle in their relationship with God, not only because of unconfessed sin in their lives, but also because they believe things that are not true (lie-based thinking) and, as a consequence, live lives of defeat and relational breakdown with God. If I have been made right and have peace with God through the Lord Jesus Christ (see Rom. 5:1) then my relationship is already in good standing, whether I feel like it is or not. If "there is . . . no condemnation for those who are in Christ" (Rom. 8:1) then I am not condemned, even if I feel that I am. Some Christians live as sin-free a life as possible; yet have minimal relational experiences with God. To have an experiential relationship with God, we have to come to know Him relationally in the same way that we know our spouse or other loved ones. I do not know my wife because I have studied about her or read books about her. I know her because I live with her and experience her daily.

In His final discourse to the church, Jesus commanded His disciples to go into the entire world with the gospel and to teach them all things (see Matt. 28:19-20) that He had taught them. The epistles instruct us to learn, grow in knowledge and mature in our understanding. Discipleship and study of God's Word play an important part in this process. Theophostic Prayer Ministry seeks to address the need for experience with God. It is not about discipleship but rather about receiving a specific truth for the displacement of a specific lie. True renewal releases us of our lie-based thinking so that we might be able to more effectively appropriate that which we logically hold to as truth yet lack supportive experience. This is not a case of either one or the other. We need to absorb the Word of God and be saturated in it, but we also need to experience the presence of Christ so that we might appropriate what we have cognitively received.

We are healed of our specific lies in a "Theophostic moment," but it is through teaching, discipleship and living life that we come into maturity in Christ. Paul declares this when he says, "we proclaim Him, admonishing every man and teaching every man with all wisdom, that we may present every man complete in Christ" (Col. 1:28).

Following this passage, Paul says, "let the word of Christ richly dwell within you, with all wisdom teaching" (Col. 3:16). Here he indicates that we are not only to study the Word, but let it richly dwell within us; let it saturate us. He told Timothy to "give attention to the public reading of Scripture, to exhortation and teaching" (1 Tim. 4:13). Scripture very clearly says that we need to study, learn, teach and grow. Theophostic Prayer Ministry does not replace this admonition to study the Word of God; it merely opens the way for our study to be more effective as we experience the presence of Jesus.

We grow in our understanding and experience of the Lord as each life situation occurs. So a Christian who is faithful and seeks the face of God will grow and mature in Christ, whether he or she ever learns of Theophostic Prayer Ministry. When we cry out to God, He shows Himself strong. It is in this experience that we shed the lies that have hindered our walk. The writer of Hebrews said we must "lay aside every encumbrance [that which weighs us down—lies?] and the sin which so easily entangles us . . . fixing our eyes on Jesus, the author and perfecter of faith" (Heb. 12:1-2).

People often tell me, "Theophostic Prayer Ministry is not new." They then say, "This happened to me years ago during a crisis in my life when . . ." They describe how their emotional pain flared up, they cried out to God and the Lord brought truth that released them of all their pain.

In our churches, we teach people biblical knowledge but they also need release from the lies that bind them. It might be better if we released them and then taught them, but at least we should do both, whichever the order may be. More information is no guarantee that people will walk in freedom. Logical truth will have difficulty overriding the power of experiential knowledge. We need experiential truth from the living Lord Jesus. Let me explain. If I am in bondage to the lie of fear in a traumatic memory, I will not likely be able to embrace the logical truth that "perfect love casts out fear" (1 John 4:18). However, when I go to the memory and embrace the fear and the lie, I am in the position to hear the specific personalized truth from the experiential presence of Jesus. When this occurs, I am then able to embrace the logical truth from the Word of God.

It requires a new experience to change or override lies learned through an old experience. If my childhood experiences have taught me that I am worthless and no good, cognitively teaching me otherwise as an adult will have little impact. You can have me memorize verses that declare that I am the righteousness of God, fully acceptable though Christ, holy and perfected in Him and I may still walk in defeat until my experiential lies are displaced with experiential divinely provided truth.

Until then, my experience will usually override my logic—unless I am able to muster up strong discipline and determination. I need an experience with Jesus that dispels these lies so that I can appropriate these logical truths and enter into maintenance-free victory.

Isn't Theophostic Prayer Ministry Just Another Form of Deliverance Ministry?

I recognize that some people need deliverance of demons but do not see battle as the means for doing so. When I am doing ministry I do not see demons as the primary problem, or exorcism as the final solution. Deliverance from demons is not the primary answer to people's emotional pain. I do believe some people are demonized, but I also know that these same demons can be sent away without any fight or resistance at the appropriate time, once the lies in people's memories are replaced with truth. This is not to say that you will not encounter demons when using Theophostic Prayer Ministry, or that demons are not having influence on those in which they inhabit.

There are several key factors that are taught in this ministry. What follows is an excerpt from the Theophostic Prayer Ministry Basic Training Seminar Manual.

• **My beliefs regarding demonization and spiritual warfare are subsidiary to the basic principles of Theophostic Prayer Ministry.** I believe it is important for counselors and ministers to know that they do not *have* to believe what I (or others) teach in this area in order to successfully administer the basics of Theophostic Prayer Ministry. This is not to say that deliverance is not important, for it is. However, I no longer stress one viewpoint of deliverance over another when doing Theophostic Prayer Ministry itself. The reality is that counselors and ministers from all venues of thought regarding spiritual warfare—even those in direct conflict with my viewpoints—are achieving good success in using the Theophostic approach.

• **Driving out the demon is not the primary goal of Theophostic Prayer Ministry because for the most part, the demon is often the symptom not the cause of the person's problem.** The focus of Theophostic Prayer Ministry is in identifying the lies one believes which are producing the emotional upheaval. If the demon in the person is not the primary problem, then deliverance from the demon is not the ultimate solution. The goal in helping demonized people should be to free them from the snare of the devil (the lie the person is holding)—of which one outcome is that the demon loses its hold and must leave. In Theophostic Prayer Ministry, deliverance is not accomplished by the minister driving out the demon but rather by his helping the person to identify why the demon is present (identifying the belief and choice of the person) and leading him or her to find truth from the Lord.

• **Since Satan was defeated through the death and resurrection of Christ 2,000 years ago, I believe we are called not to fight a defeated foe but rather to stand in the *full armor of God,* which is the finished work of Christ.** The armor listed in Ephesians 6:10-18 must be understood in the light of the overriding message of the Apostle's letter—our triumphant position in Christ and not one of battle. This is especially clear in the first chapter where Paul states, "He raised Him from the dead and seated Him at His right hand in the heavenly places, *far above* all rule and authority and power and dominion, and every name that is named, not only in this age but also in the one to come. And He put all things in subjection under His feet, and gave Him as head over *all things to the church,* which is His body, *the fullness of Him* who fills all in all" (Eph. 1:20-23). The authority over the enemy that was given to Christ has also been given to the Church!

• **Defeat does not render the devil brain dead; thus he is still actively at work in the hearts of the "sons of disobedience" and seeks to deceive and devour the believer who does not walk in truth.** Though Satan has lost his position of power, he is still very capable of deceiving those who are not "on the alert." Now, however, a primary weapon he uses against us is his deceptive schemes. In the few places in the post-resurrection passages where struggle with the devil is said to be evident, the focus is on the schemes of the devil and not the devil himself (see Eph. 6:11). Some might suggest that if Satan is indeed powerless then he should not be able to deceive us either. Deception has nothing to do with power. Power means, "I can cause something to happen because I am powerful." Power gives me the ability to make you do something that you do not willfully choose to do. Satan does not have the power to make me do anything I do not willfully choose at some level of my thinking. Whereas, deception occurs when I am able to influence or manipulate another into making something happen when in fact I may be powerless to bring it about myself alone. Even so, Satan has been acting as a master of deception drawing many into his snares from the beginning and will continue up until his demise at the Lord's appointed time. In the meantime we live in an evil world. However, before we give Satan more credit than is due him. it is important to note that every act of evil in this world is accomplished as a result of a human's choice. Satan really is powerless to accomplish any evil apart from human participation. Demon's instigate, manipulate and motivate but evil outcome requires people's cooperation.

• **Satan does not hold the same position today in the post-resurrection time period as he did prior to the cross**. When Adam sinned, he surrendered the authority he had been given to rule over the earth to the devil (see Gen. 1:28; Luke 4:6). However, when Christ, the last Adam, offered Himself up for our sins, He restored redeemed man to his former position of authority over Satan in this world (see 1 Cor. 15:45; Heb. 7:27). We are now "seated us with Him [Christ] in the heavenly places" (Eph. 2:6). The proper perspective for viewing and understanding the devil in the world today is from the post-resurrection Scriptures. It is in this context that Satan is operating not from the position he held prior to the cross.

• **Demonization in the individual is directly related to the person's belief system and ultimate choosing.** This is not to say that a demonized person is choosing to be demonized but that the demonization is resting on the individual's belief and choices. While deliverance from demons can occur with a frontal attack that sidesteps the person's belief and choice (my approach in years past), the person will still remain in bondage to the lies from which the demons were operating. Casting out demons does not deal with the lie structures (belief systems) to which the demons attach themselves to and operate within. Deliverance, apart from people dealing with their own deception and its consequent choices, shortchanges the fuller plan of God for their lives (renewed minds). Since the demon's primary hold on a person is the person's own beliefs and choices, I approach each demonic encounter with the question "Why is this demon here?" not with "How do I drive it out?" The answer to the "why it is here" is found in the deceptions (lies) the person has hold of and the consequential choices he is making. It is my continuing experience that demons will do exactly as they are told *without any battle* when we operate in the experiential truth of who we are in Christ *and* if the demonized person genuinely *wills it to be so*. If a counselor or minister finds he is fighting with the devil in a ministry session, then he is not acting in the fullness of his or her authority or else the person's will runs contrary to the deliverance. True authority and the ministry recipient's willful choice for freedom, bypasses the need for battle. If a demon refuses to comply when confronted with genuine authority, it is because the demonized person has a "belief and will" problem permitting the demon to maintain its hold. Some might suggest that the reason for the demon's hold is sin. I agree that in some cases this is so, but sin is also the consequence of belief and choice—I believe something, I make a choice, and then I sin.

Demons do not hold people captive against their will but rather in accordance with what the person believes to be experientially true. When the one held captive by the snare of the devil comes into the knowledge of the truth the result is that the person comes to his or her senses and walks out of the snare without any battle. Paul instructed Timothy with these words when dealing with people held in a demonic snare, "with gentleness correcting those who are in opposition, if perhaps God may grant them repentance [literally, change of thinking] leading to the knowledge [literally, experiential knowing] of the truth, and they may come to their senses [literally, sober up] *and escape* from the snare of the devil, having been held captive by him to do his will" (2 Tim. 2:25-26). When I step into a snare my captivity is the snare not the snarer himself. My freedom comes when the snare (deception) is removed and I see my way clear (come to my senses) to make truth-based choices.

I used to restate myself, give my commands over and over, speak louder and more emphatically, quote more Scripture, claim the blood or bring out the olive oil. Now I never answer a demon's question, never give a command twice, make each command clear with no loop-holes or alternative interpretations and make the lie-based thinking the focus.

As a weary warrior, I left my sword at the tomb many years ago and today still enjoy resting in the Lord's victory and watching many people come into the truth, find peace and have their lives transformed without fighting the devil on their behalf. The approach to spiritual warfare I am sharing here is without question bearing genuine fruit.

Satan and all his demons were defeated and remain defeated through the death of Christ. The victory is secure. All we have to do now is to *stand* in truth and *resist* the devil's schemes. Ephesians 6 focuses the struggle, on the schemes of the devil and not on the devil himself. The apostle Paul declares that the devil could not take advantage of him since he was "not ignorant of his schemes" (2 Cor. 2:11). Ignorance not only puts us at a disadvantage, but is also the seedbed where much demonic activity is germinated and comes to fruition. If we believe something to be true (even though it is not), then what we believe becomes *experientially* true to us and becomes the parameters in which demons are allowed to operate. This sounds like the Theophostic principle that says, *If you believe a lie then it may as well be the truth since the consequences will be much the same.*

When dealing with a demon, always know that it is only present in the person's life due to something that the person believes and is making willful choices upon. As you identify the false belief and the Lord reveals His truth you will witness how powerless these creatures actually are as they fall off without any struggle on your part or the person's.

• **Demonized people should not be viewed as helpless victims that need to be rescued from the devil.** It is also important how we view demonized people. Rather than being helpless victims of the devil, they should be seen as people void of some element of the truth. In this unfortunate state they are thus deceived and held captive by the snare of the devil as opposed to being held captive by the snarer himself (see 2 Tim. 2:26). I do not need to beat the devil off of someone, but rather to pray that God might grant change of thinking [repentance], leading to the knowledge of the truth so that they might come to their senses, having escaped the snare of the devil, having been held captive to do his will (see 2 Tim. 2:25-26). If we believe we have to fight demons and rescue their victims held captive, then the demons are more than willing to put up a fight. If we believe we have to wear demons down before they will leave, we will wrestle with them endlessly. Such battling bestows on them the attention they crave, and even though they are defeated, Satan is given glory, having been elevated again to a power he no longer has. However, as we come into experiential knowledge that we have the same authority over the enemy as Jesus Himself, we will discover that demons do exactly as they are commanded (see Eph. 1:20-23).

Does Theophostic Prayer Ministry Take a Soft Position on Sin and Make the Sinner Out to Be a Poor Victim of His or Her Circumstances?

To answer this question I've adapted the following material from the Basic Seminar Manual.

Sometimes the pain people carry is not the result of having been unjustly wounded, but is coming from a self-inflicted wound or sin. In these times, people suffer emotional pain due to their own choice rather than as a result of what someone else has done to them. I am referring to willful acts of sin.

When I use the word sin, I am referring to any behavior we engage in as a result of choices that we make that are less than God's ideal desire for our lives. These sinful choices are often vain attempts to relieve us of emotional pain or by acting this pain out in a sinful manner. For example, I might act out my pain by defending myself with harsh words if someone triggered my lies of inadequacy. I might try to comfort myself for feeling worthless by eating food even though I am not hungry.

The word for sin most often used in the New Testament is the Greek word *harmatia*, which means, in its basic understanding, to miss the mark. When we seek to heal ourselves, we miss the mark and never know the full restoration God intends for us. Sin may also be the initial response we have carried of anger or hate toward the one who wounded us. This reaction was predictable and righteous when the event occurred (see Eph. 4:26), but this same anger is destructive and deceiving for us who continue to carry it (see Eph. 4:31). Many who have been wounded believe the anger they hold benefits them and empowers them. The opposite is true. This reactionary anger must be dealt with and forsaken if they are ever to know complete release.

Some have suggested that to overcome sin we simply need to confess it, turn from it and choose to obey God. This is a traditional view but is it really any different than keeping the Law? Many people are in this cycle of defeat and see no way free.

This approach has, at its foundation, overcoming sin as the solution. It has also forgotten that the only cure for sin is the cross of Christ. It is implied that if we overcome sin (which we cannot do), we would walk in victory. I want to suggest that if we focus on sin as the only problem and do not address the lies behind the sin, we set ourselves up for ultimate defeat and a cycle of perpetual confession, repentance and performance-based spirituality. Though this is a common practice in the Church and most other world religions, it has afforded limited success except from the ones most disciplined. Sin is always precluded by a thought. This thought is based on a deception at some level. The lie is present in every sinful choice and act we make. If the lie is not identified and removed, the sin will perpetually and predictably resurface when the pain is triggered.

The truth is, we have to think before we act out sinfully. I am suggesting that if we can find freedom from the lies we experientially believe, we are less likely to think sinfully and therefore less prone to sin. I have lie-based thinking that gets triggered; this stirs up a bad feeling; I have to decide to either express the pain, cover the pain or go to the source of the pain as is advocated with Theophostic Prayer Ministry. If I do not go to the source and find truth, I must then make a choice as to whether I will act it out or not.

As I mentioned in an earlier chapter, according to James 1:14-15 the sin process flows in a predictable fashion. First, the enemy provides a temptation or life situation, which is tailored to trigger an original thought or experiential lie. The experiential lie is a belief, which was received during the life experience. We may or may not consciously think the original lie or thought in our current situation, but nevertheless it is aroused. For example, if we are raised in an alcoholic home, we might learn a belief such as, "Life is out of control and I am responsible to do something to remove the chaos." Once the original thought is triggered and stirred, a matching emotion will emerge. Now we feel out of control. The enemy then provides a workable solution to deal with the feelings of being out of control. He might suggest we go to the refrigerator and binge, read a pornographic magazine, clean the house, yell at the kids, jog around the block, go to church, etc. We now act on the enemy's solution and the painful, anxious or fearful emotions are masked until the original lie is triggered again. In the meantime we may feel guilty for the choice we have made, so we confess our sin, repent and promise not to do it again. We may be successful for a time, but at some point the lie and its emotion will find their way back through our behavior.

Often victory is falsely equated with the cessation of a particular behavior and its replacement with a more acceptable one. For example, we may stop compulsive eating or not eating by replacing it with daily jogging (as is often the case with anorexia). We might quit drinking and overcompensate with religious behavior. Any attempt to overcome our lie-based pain by adjusting our behavior is works based sanctification, not faith and grace. The lie still remains and the emotions driving the compulsion are merely routed through a different avenue.

I am not belittling the power and the destructive reality of sin in one's life. Sinful behavior must be contended with, but if overcoming it through self-effort and controlling behavior becomes the focus for finding victory, defeat is inevitable since the only cure for sin is the cross of Christ.[3]

Will Theophostic Prayer Ministry Work with a Person Who Does Not Know Christ?

There are many people now in the kingdom of God because they found peace in their minds though the administering of Theophostic Prayer Ministry and then were introduced to their Healer and thus trusted Him to redeem them through faith by grace. When the nonbeliever finds grace from God, he or she very well may become highly motivated to move into an eternal relationship with God through faith in the redemptive work of Christ. This happened often in the Gospels. Jesus did not require a life commitment from those He healed. Yet many came to be His followers and worshipped Him, once they received His physical healing. The blind man did not even know who Jesus was until after he received his sight and was thrown out of the temple. Later he discovered Jesus' identity and worshipped Him.

Some have mistakenly believed the notion that God will not hear or speak to a nonbeliever in Christ. If this is true, then why did God in the flesh (Jesus) find it easy to have fellowship and converse with the sinner? Jesus was very comfortable in conversing and ministering to the sinners and nonbelievers of His day. The truth is Jesus had a hard time communicating and having fellowship with the so-called righteous in the Gospel stories.

Just a few weeks ago a lady came to my house to discuss some business issues. She was not a believer. After our business matters were settled I asked her how she was doing in her personal life. She reported that she was having a difficult time in her life. I asked a few more questions and she began to open up to me and deep pain began to surface. I shared with her the basic Theophostic principles and then asked her if she would like to be free of this pain. She said she would.

I did not initially talk about Jesus, the church, her need for salvation or the apparent sin in her life. I simply invited her to feel the emotions that she was feeling. A painful childhood memory surfaced. We identified the reason for the pain (the lies she believed) and I asked her to simply report whatever she saw, sensed or heard as I asked the Lord to reveal His truth to her. After a few moments she responded with truths that had come into her thinking. I asked her to try to find the pain that was present when we started the process. She reported that it was all gone and that she felt real good (that translates into perfect peace). I asked her where the truth that she had received had come from. She said it was from God. I asked her if she would like to have the same peace in her heart that she was feeling in her mind, and she was eager to receive the Lord Jesus.

It is important to note that mind renewal does not constitute salvation. A person can have renewing of the mind and still be eternally separated from God. I have had the privilege of leading people to a saving knowledge of the Lord Jesus by first offering them His renewing grace before I try to talk to them about their eternal destiny. I simply begin where the person is — in pain. This is the same place Jesus often started when ministering to people. As people find peace in their minds, the possibility of peace in their hearts becomes very appealing. If someone struggles with the idea that lost people can be recipients of truth then I would suggest that he simply not minister to lost people using this approach. Embracing this idea is non-essential for doing this ministry.

Is It Possible That My Life Will Become More Painful if I Open Up the Hidden Places of Pain in My Memories?

Some have suggested that people who receive this form of ministry actually get worse before they get better. This is sometimes the truth. It was true for me, though it was not because Theophostic Prayer Ministry causes more pain. It was because my emotional pain had been repressed and the painful emotions were finally being released. I did not know that I was carrying repressed anger and rage due to hundreds of childhood experiences where I was not permitted to be angry. It was not until I began to allow the Holy Spirit to take me to these hidden places that my rage and anger surfaced. Up until this time I had actually been proud that I had always controlled my anger. I saw this controlled behavior as spiritual prowess, when in fact it was a childhood defense against pain. I am excited to say that after many ministry sessions I have far less anger to surface. Even though I felt worse before I felt better, I am thoroughly enjoying the peace on this side of the journey. It was definitely worth the trip.

If you are carrying pain that you are hesitant to uncover for fear that it will get worse before it gets better, remember that it is Jesus who awaits you on the other side with His perfect peace. It is also Jesus who will walk with you every step along the way. "Be anxious for nothing, but in everything by prayer and supplication with thanksgiving let your requests be made known to God. And the peace of God, which surpasses all comprehension shall guard your hearts and your minds in Christ Jesus" (Phil. 4:6-7).

Is Theophostic Prayer Ministry Just Another Form of Recovered Memory Therapy?

What is Recovered Memory Therapy?
Those who practice Recovered Memory Therapy believe that dysfunctional symptoms are almost always rooted in a repressed traumatic memory, and that people's repressed memories can only be uncovered using such techniques as symptoms check-off lists, group dynamics, visualization, hypnosis, trance writing, dream interpretation, body massage, drugs, relaxation therapy, and spirit guides. They believe that by exposing their

clients' repressed memories through the use of these techniques, the symptomologies will be resolved.

Theophostic Prayer Ministry does not practice any of these techniques listed here. However, Theophostic Prayer Ministry does believe (as do most other venues of ministry and counseling) that most people's present emotional duress is rooted in what they believe, and that negative thinking results in unhealthy mental and spiritual choices and consequences. This is the essence of Cognitive Therapy. Theophostic Prayer Ministry holds that people tend to feel and act out what they have their minds set on — as described in Proverb 23:7, *"For as a man thinks in his heart, so is he,"* (NKJV) and in Romans 8:5-6, *"Those who are according to the flesh set their minds on the things of the flesh, but those who are according to the Spirit, the things of the Spirit. For the mind set on the flesh is death, but the mind set on the Spirit is life and peace."*

Theophostic Prayer Ministry has as one of its goals to expose falsehood (lies) and replace it with God's truth. In fact, the same biblical perspective is held by many other professional and pastoral counselors who knowingly or unknowingly practice some type of cognitive therapy in their efforts to identify faulty thinking and replace it with truth.

One important distinction between Theophostic Prayer Ministry (and most other cognitive counseling methods) and Recovered Memory Therapy is in how people's memories are accessed and how the truth is distributed. Theophostic Prayer Ministry focuses more on discovering the false belief contained in a memory experience than on exploring the memory itself. Theophostic Prayer Ministry seeks to help people receive and assimilate the renewal truth that God reveals to them, not just to expose the memory content. In contrast, Recovered Memory Therapy appears to view the uncovering of the supposed repression as the means of achieving resolution, which, if that is all that occurs, may leave the person in a worse emotional state than he was in *before* his discovery. Simply uncovering a memory does not bring any real resolution, since the pain in the memory is rooted in the lies contained therein and not the memory itself. Simply uncovering a repressed memory (along with the person abreacting) does not promise any level of resolution or recovery. Resolution occurs when people receive truth from God.

Distinctions between Recovered Memory Therapy and TPM

There are several distinctions between the basic techniques used in Recovered Memory Therapy and Theophostic Prayer Ministry. Each of the basic techniques of Recovered Memory Therapy listed below is followed by an explanation of how Theophostic Prayer Ministry differs. This is not an exhausted list of RMT techniques, but it covers the primary ones.

• *Recovered Memory Therapy sometimes uses a "check-off" list of symptoms.* The check-off list includes symptoms that are believed to indicate the presence of repressed memory. Examples are: Do you have an aversion to sex? Do you feel uncomfortable in enclosed places? Do you have a fear of water? Does the number 666 bother you?

• *The Theophostic process does NOT utilize any symptoms check-off list.* There was an emotion identification chart supplied in an earlier edition of the TPM Basic Seminar Manual that was used by some using Theophostic Prayer Ministry. This chart was used to help the person better identify what he or she is presently feeling, but is not a listing of questions or symptoms as found in RMT. Instead, people are asked to identify the emotional pain in their lives and seek to discover its source. The source is usually a false belief that was learned in a real life experience and is now stored in a consciously held memory. This process is quite similar to the cognitive approaches typically used in biblical counseling.

• *Recovered Memory Therapy seems to assume that recovering repressed memory is essential to symptomatic improvement.* It is said of RMT therapists that they seem to accept the premise that ALL symptoms indicate repression.

• *Theophostic Prayer Ministry holds to the belief that painful emotions, dysfunctional behavior, and many disorders (eating, personality, etc.) may have sources that are rooted in faulty thinking.* It assumes that bad symptoms are generally connected to bad thinking, whether conscious or repressed.[1] Since it is probable that some of the faulty thinking of some people is rooted in repressed memory, logic would tell us that if a person's faulty thinking is rooted in repressed memory, it needs to be exposed and replaced with truth before his or her symptomology can change. But—and this is crucial—Theophostic Prayer Ministry does NOT hold that symptomatic improvement occurs because repressed memories are recovered. It holds, rather, that symptomatic improvement occurs when the lies in either repressed or conscious memories are exposed and replaced with truth. Merely uncovering a person's painful memories will have no real impact on reducing the discomfort. In fact, it is likely that, unless the lies in the memories are resolved with truth, simply uncovering the painful memories will further intensify the person's problems. Theophostic Prayer Ministry teaches that it is not the traumatic event itself that sustains the painful emotion the person feels; rather, the persistent negative emotions come from the person's lie-based interpretations of the original event.

• *RMT often uses group therapy, putting people with similar issues and symptoms together.* It is possible that in the context of RMT group therapy, the soil is cultivated for the implantation of "false memory" into the minds of the new participants. As new group participants who have not yet come into the knowledge of their supposed repression mix with those who have already reported repressed memory, the abuse stories and memory content of the more progressed members are accepted by the new members as their own.[1]

• *Theophostic Prayer Ministry does not advocate using group therapy when administering the Theophostic process.* This is not to say that group dynamics do not have value in their proper context. However, Theophostic Prayer Ministry does not hold to the belief that people need to discuss their personal struggles/historical wounds in a support group in order to receive emotional renewal and healing. The Theophostic method encourages individuals to embrace the emotional pain they are carrying and discover the lies underlying the pain. Theophostic Prayer Ministry focuses on the individual's specific lie-based issue(s) with the goal of helping him or her experience a personal encounter with the living presence of Christ.

• *Recovered Memory Therapy utilizes visualization techniques to achieve age regression.* These techniques tend to be hypnotic in nature. For example, the therapist might ask his client to envision himself entering an upper elevator and descending floor by floor toward the basement—the descent representing regression to earlier ages. The intent is to uncover the repressed memories stored in early childhood events. The lower the person descends, the younger he becomes.

• *Theophostic Prayer Ministry views visualization as a questionable therapy technique and opposes its use.* Theophostic facilitators do NOT encourage their ministry recipients to create mind imagery to be used as a vehicle for time travel. However, Theophostic Prayer Ministry is founded on the principle that a person's present emotional pain is often not solely rooted in his or her present circumstances. While the person's current circumstances may contribute to his or her emotional distress, the emotional responses that surface day after day are generally rooted in unresolved lie-based memories (either conscious or repressed) that are triggered by events of a similar type in the current life situation. For example, a woman who has a painful emotional reaction (i.e., panic attack) to her husband's sexual advances may be "triggered" by something she believes about sex that is contained in an historical real-life event. If this is the case, the negative emotion she feels in the current situation can act as an "emotional smoke trail" she can follow back to its lie-based source.

It is important to note here that all cognitive activity is rooted in memory. Apart from the present moment, all experience is past tense and can be known only through memory. This means that no matter what method a therapist uses, he has no option but to deal with memory. If I am working with a married couple about their relationship I have no choice but talk with them about what has already happened (memory) in order to deal with what the might do to avoid future conflict. Memory is really all we have apart from the immeasurable moment we call the present. So the issue under consideration here is what method is used to help the person deal with his or her past? While Recovered Memory Therapy encourages the use of visualization techniques, Theophostic Prayer Ministry helps the person identify his or her current painful emotion and follow it back to its lie-based memory source, where the lie can be replaced with God's truth.

• *Recovered Memory Therapy sometimes uses "trance writing" or "inner child journaling."* Sometimes these practices take place during hypnosis. The client is given a pen and encouraged to allow his or her supposed "inner child" to express hidden memories and feelings in drawings. The therapist then examines the drawings to discern what might be the presence of a repressed memory.

• *Theophostic Prayer Ministry does not advocate any practices such as this.* In Theophostic, people are not encouraged to get in touch with their "inner child." However, if such manifestation occurs it is not rejected if it is the person's own origination. There is no use of hypnosis. Neither is journaling employed during ministry sessions (although journaling can be valuable in its proper context). Instead, people are encouraged to learn to listen to what they are really thinking and saying to themselves in order to discover what it is they believe that is producing the emotional distress in their lives.

• *Recovered Memory Therapy sometimes uses body massage in order to release hidden memory.* The therapist massages the area of the body where he believes the cells have stored the memory of a particular trauma. The practice is based on the premise that traumatic memory is stored in body cells and needs to be released to the brain in order for the person to get emotional resolution.

• *Theophostic Prayer Ministry does not advocate or use any form of massage therapy.*

• *Recovery Memory Therapy utilizes dream interpretation.* Dream interpretation is often used in the context of hypnotherapy. The person may be hypnotized and asked to replay the dream, which the therapist then interprets in regard to possible repressed trauma and abuse.

• *Theophostic Prayer Ministry strongly discourages any interpretation of dreams, visual images, inner thoughts, etc., that could provide the person with false information.* The facilitator is taught to avoid adding any personal input regarding any aspect of a person's memory content. He works only with the information that the person surfaces on his own. For a more detailed understanding of the role of the facilitator, read the TPM Guidelines.

• *Recovered Memory Therapy sometimes uses drugs such as sodium amatol to aid in memory recovery.* Sodium amatol is a barbiturate drug (truth serum) that produces an altered state of deep relaxation in the client. After administering the drug, the therapist will question the person about his past, using age regression techniques to probe for assumed suppressed memories.

• *Theophostic Prayer Ministry NEVER uses any drugs in any form for any purpose.*

• *Recovered Memory Therapy may suggest using "spirit guides" to lead people to his or her repressed memories.* The person is told to look for a personal spirit guide along the pathway he envisions leading into the hidden places of his or her mind. The spirit guide is to aid him or her by revealing hidden "truths" about the past. At some point the person may report meeting a spirit guide — who may even say he is Jesus.

• *Theophostic Prayer Ministry opposes this practice as total deception and probably demonically driven.* Theophostic Prayer Ministry views any spirit guide (even a "Jesus") that a person encounters in such practice as a demonic spirit — nothing more than either an evil impersonator of good who will ultimately lead the person into deception or a fabrication of the person's mind. This practice falls in the same category as channeling, and is totally repudiated by Theophostic Prayer Ministry.

• *Recovered Memory Therapy uses relaxation therapy techniques. The therapist may have the person visualize a quiet, safe place where he can let down his defenses and relax.* It is while the person is in this relaxed and susceptible state that the therapist may offer memory suggestions.

• *Theophostic Prayer Ministry does not engage people in any form of relaxation therapy.* People receiving ministry are NEVER told to visualize anything or imagine being in any place other than in the chair in which they are seated. They are not told to relax or calm down or seek a place in their mind that is peaceful. To the contrary, they are encouraged to focus on their absence of peace (if this is the case) and move toward the place in their thinking that is causing the discomfort. They are encouraged to feel the painful emotions, not escape them. They are encouraged to focus on the pain they are feeling and go to where they are willing and where God empowers with courage to go.

Summary

Theophostic Prayer Ministry is unapologetic in its use of focused prayer. Theophostic Prayer Ministry is prayer ministry. Those who charge the Theophostic process (closed eyes, inward focus on feeling and thinking) with being a form of hypnosis or a relaxation technique must concede that all religions that promote prayer and meditation are guilty of the same practices. As Christians, we are told to cast all of our anxiety on Jesus (1 Peter 5:7) — to own what we feel and cast it on Jesus. In the Scriptures where we are told to "be still and know that [He is] God," we are not considered to be practicing hypnosis. This owning, feeling, and casting our anxieties on Jesus is essentially what Theophostic Prayer Ministry is about. As we focus on Him and allow Him to renew our thinking with His truth, we are able to enter into His peace and walk in His victory.

Chapter Eight

What to Expect in a Session

Be Discerning

Ironically, an unfair rule exists that says a ministry will be judged not by what it teaches or its founding principles, but rather by the results of those least capable or qualified to perform the ministry. In other words, even though tens of thousands have reported Theophostic Prayer Ministry to be a highly effective ministry tool to bring about lasting renewal and change in people, it is sometimes defined by the reports of the nightmare sessions facilitated by the most ill-equipped trainees. This is unfortunate but true. A few horror stories have surfaced from people who went to receive what they thought was to be a Theophostic Prayer Ministry session and were hurt even more as a consequence. I am happy to say that of all the thousands of emails we receive, only a very small number are negative. Almost all of the negative reports come from unfortunate situations where people simply did not follow the training guidelines and basic principles.

242

However, if research could be obtained concerning any other form of ministry or counseling, you would find the same negative reports surfacing. To keep a proper perspective of things, the few negative reports that have surfaced need to be viewed in light of the enormous swell of thousands of positive testimonies that come in continually from all around the world.

Theophostic Prayer Ministry seeks to encourage people to operate within the parameters of their training, expertise and qualifications. Lay ministers are encouraged to work under the supervision of those more qualified and mental health professionals are encouraged to network with the lay ministries so that most effective ministry can be achieved. Genuine ministry is not about us and them (lay ministers and professionals) but rather the Body of Christ coming together to form a unified force against the evil bondages we are all faced with. Since we are one body, when one of us suffers we all suffer and when one is deceived and ensnared we are all held captive. No one is completely free until we all find freedom.

Theophostic Prayer Ministry also acknowledges that completing the Basic Training offered by this ministry does not qualify any person to be a counselor, minister or anything other than being trained in this ministry approach. Lay ministers and other non-professionals are strongly encouraged to seek training in other areas of helping ministry in order to become all that one can be for the cause of Christ.

Questions to Ask

If you desire authentic Theophostic Prayer Ministry, you need to be able to discern whether the person ministering to you is following the basic principles outlined in the Basic Training Seminar. Now and then we have people call in and complain that what they received in a Theophostic Prayer Ministry session did not work. For the most part, we tend to discover either a person trying to do Theophostic Prayer Ministry who was ill equipped to do so, someone who was not following the principles as they are taught or someone that simply should not be doing ministry period. What follow are some questions you may want to ask of the person offering Theophostic Prayer Ministry before submitting to his or her care.

Will you be guiding or directing the process?
People trained in the Theophostic principles are taught *not* to tell you where to go in your memories, not ask leading questions or tell you what you should experience. This process is God directed and God enlightened. Jesus does not need our insight or help in setting people free from their lies. He allows us to

participate in the journey by leading a person to the place where he or she is able to receive, but the transmission of truth must come from Jesus alone.

Do you use any form of directed imagery or guided visualization?

Jesus will reveal truth to you in whatever form He chooses. You may have little to no visualization in this process, which is fine. No one should tell you what you will see or if you will see anything. The one doing ministry with you should not suggest imagery to you. For example, a person should not ask Jesus to do anything for you in the process, such as hold you, take you out of the painful memory, put the pain in a box or take the pain away. This is not Theophostic Prayer Ministry. However, the minister may ask Jesus questions that are reflective of what you are seeing or experiencing, or may simply ask Him what He wants to do in the memory context. For example, if you reported that you were feeling alone and abandoned, the facilitator might ask Jesus, "What do You want her to know in this memory about why she feels this way?" If you describe a scene where something is happening, the facilitator might ask the Lord, "Is there something in this memory that she still needs to see, understand or feel?" If you are having a hard time discerning what you believe in the memory, the facilitator might ask Jesus, "What is it in this memory that she believes that is causing her this pain?" When the way is not clear or you do not know what to do, asking Jesus for guidance, direction or clarity is the right thing to do.

Will you be telling me what you believe is happening during the session?

If you are in the memory, the person doing ministry should only help you discern the lies and invite Jesus to reveal His truth. No one should tell you what he or she thinks God wants you to know. The minister's job is to help you reach the place where you are able to discern the lie you are believing and feel its pain, but then the minister should step aside and invite Jesus to reveal the truth you need.

Will you be asking me leading questions or statements?

If the minister has an idea or thinks he knows about what may have happened to you, he or she should never suggest it or ask questions that cause you to think in any direction other than what your mind has revealed to you. As mentioned previously, asking questions of you or of Jesus is perfectly acceptable, as long as the questions are reflective of what has been revealed by you the recipient and not the insight or thinking of the facilitator. To ask questions about that which has not been surfaced by you would be to mislead and possibly misdirect the process.

In addition to the above questions you might want to ask these background questions before you go through a session with a new facilitator.

• Have you been through the Basic Video Training Seminar, which includes watching all video sessions and having read the entire 400-plus pages of training materials?

• Are you using the Theophostic principles as your primary means of ministry? (Be careful of those who are mixing other approaches with Theophostic Prayer Ministry. If they are, ask if they are using any forms of creative imagery, hypnosis, visualization or other counselor-directive methods. I am not suggesting that other forms of ministry are not effective, because some are. You will need to decide what you want if the one offering you ministry is using other approaches along with Theophostic Prayer Ministry.)

• To how many people have you ministered Theophostic principles where you saw significant freedom using this approach? (Everyone has to start with his first person. The question is, do you want to be his first?)

• Have you experienced renewal yourself with this process, and are you continuing this renewal? (Something is wrong if the person isn't receiving renewal him- or herself and submitting to ministry.

We all need this ministry. Those who have received ministry are usually better at ministering to others.)

• Have you continued your study beyond the Basic Training materials and were the Basic Training materials you used printed before the year 2000? (There have been major revisions that far exceeds the previous edition of the Basic Training in 1999.)

• Are you under the authority and spiritual covering of a recognized ministry, church or professional Christian organization? (If the person is operating as a lone wolf, be careful. Check out his or her ministry through other established ministries in the area, if possible. Ask for references from those in the area who can give a positive endorsement.)

Be responsible to pray about and discern those from whom you seek ministry. If at any point you feel uncomfortable with what is happening, simply stop the session and decide what it is you need or desire from the person doing the ministry.

Included in this book is a copy of the Theophostic Prayer Ministry Guidelines. These guidelines are designed to provide the ministry recipient with an overview of what a ministry session should look like. If you are seeking Theophostic Prayer Ministry use this sheet to evaluate what happens in your session. You should also take this sheet with you to your session and ask the person if this is what they intend to follow.

I encourage those seeking ministry to carefully check out those who are offering ministry before they submit to a session. Never assume that people offering ministry necessarily know what they are doing, or that they are doing Theophostic Prayer Ministry simply because they say they are. If you go to a person who is claiming to be using Theophostic Prayer Ministry, feel free to make a copy of the Theophostic Prayer Ministry Guidelines and have him or her complete it before your first session. This will give you some measure of assurance that the counselor is at least on the right page before you begin.

Is Theophostic Prayer Ministry effective in all cases?

I personally have witnessed what appears to be genuine resolve for a host of people over the past ten years. Also, over the last few years, thousands of testimonies and reports have flooded into the Theophostic office proclaiming life transformation as a result of encountering Christ. As I have contacted many of these people in follow up, they have reported that the peace of Christ is still present in their former places of pain. I am very excited about what the Lord is doing in and through this ministry. However, I do hear reports now and then from some facilitators and ministry recipients who say that this ministry did not work for them personally. I truly desire that all people find their way to the peace of Christ that God has promised. Although I do not have any decisive answers as to why Theophostic Prayer Ministry does not seem to help all people, I offer up the following possibilities:

1) *Not everything that is being offered and called Theophostic Prayer Ministry is indeed Theophostic Prayer Ministry.* Some of what is being called Theophostic Prayer Ministry is a little of this and a little of that and not too much of what is defined as genuine Theophostic. Ministry recipients need to BEWARE of what they are receiving by way of ministry. This is why it is very important that the recipient of ministry be educated in the basic teachings of this ministry before seeking personal ministry. Never assume that just because people say they are doing Theophostic that they are. A minimum requirement for every ministry recipient would be that he or she read this book and obtain and carefully read a copy of the TPM Session Guidelines. There is also a facilitator evaluation/questionnaire on the web site and in this book that the ministry recipient should have the facilitator complete before receiving ministry. This evaluation will give the ministry recipient a snapshot of

what the facilitator should be doing. (The guidelines and evaluation follow at the end of this chapter.) If anywhere along the way the ministry recipient is not pleased with what is happening, he or she should stop what is occurring and seek ministry elsewhere.

2) *The expertise and skill level of the ministry facilitator may not be up to par.*

Just because people have read the training materials and attended a Basic Training Seminar does not mean they have developed the intuitive ability to minister effectively that comes only with much practice and thus increases success. The Basic Training seminar Manual is almost 400 pages long and is packed with many principles, concepts and ideas. There are many hours of video training sessions as well. After reading and viewing the training materials, supervision and practice is needed to become adequately equipped. It would be good for ministry recipients to find out how much experience the facilitator has had and what his or her success rate has been. Every facilitator has to begin with a first person, but the question is whether or not the level of experience that the facilitator is at meets the needs of the person receiving ministry. This is something that should be considered by both facilitators and ministry recipients before deciding to work together.

3) *The ministry recipient may not be at a place where he is ready to embrace the pain in his life.*

I have found that some of the deepest and most painful places of my renewal journey have only opened up to me in the last year (after eight years of receiving ministry.) I did not realize that I was not ready to allow the Lord to expose these places. I am learning more and more that this journey is about God saving me from myself and from the highly developed defenses I have erected. I have developed an amazing structure of mental defenses to bury and block out the pain in my life. These defenses are actually keeping me in bondage and not protecting at all. My freedom has come only because of the Lord's faithfulness to orchestrate my life in such a way that I have been motivated to look at why I am in pain. There have been numerous places where I did not even know I was carrying pain. The greatest example has been in my suppressed anger. I once prided myself in my spiritual ability to not express anger. The truth was that I was filled with rage in many unresolved places that God exposed when I was finally willing and ready to admit it. Being angry and yet keeping it suppressed is not a spiritual virtue or an indication of spiritual prowess. It was much more difficult to admit and allow my anger to surface than it was to keep it hidden. I have found this to be true in many other people's lives as well. This is especially true in cases where there is the defense of dissociation present keeping people from moving into the painful places in their minds. When we are unwilling to move in the direction of the painful lies we hold we will remain stuck and this process will not "work."

4) *It is possible that this process may not work for some people because God has a different renewal path laid out for them.* Theophostic is not the "magic bullet" for all people but there is a path through which God can accomplish His work if we are walking on it. God is certainly not limited to this ministry approach even though I am seeing more consistent results that ever before in my own life and ministry. For those who have not had success using this approach to ministry (and have considered what I just mentioned in the points listed above), I would encourage you to diligently seek the Lord and see where He is leading you. Pursue other avenues of ministry and help. Keep knocking and believing that the Lord will open the door in His time. Please do not sit down and play the martyr for He does have a plan that is specific for you. When I hear someone say to me, "Theophostic Prayer Ministry just does not work for me" I want to ask, "What then is it that you are doing that is working?" God is at work in His children and when there is no evidence of this work then either we are not his children or we are hindering the sanctification process in some way ourselves. If Theophostic Prayer Ministry is not working

then some other means of help should be working or there is a problem. If we are not continually moving in the direction of God's healing grace and sanctification then we are making a choice somewhere not to move. I do not mean to sound condescending or shaming but do encourage everyone to pursue God with all his or her heart, mind and strength for God does want to renew all of us and reveal Himself to us. He has called us to come to Him in faith where He desires to restore us and make us whole. *"For without faith it is impossible to please Him, for he who _comes to God must believe that He is and that He is a rewarder of those who seek Him"* (Heb. 11:6).

5) *Some people have misunderstood what this ministry has claimed about what it can do and cannot do.*

There have been critics who have said that we made certain claims that we have never made. We have never suggested that people are completely made whole within their minds simply by participating in a few sessions. We have clearly taught that renewal occurs memory-by-memory and lie-by lie, over the course of a lifetime. I don't believe that a single session of this ministry will resolve all the pain in a person's life, since mind renewal is a lifelong journey. It would be marvelous if this were so in that I often grow weary of the journey and would love a quick fix. I am a landfill of lies and rarely does a day pass that I am not exposed to more of what is not true in my thinking. However, just because a person still has emotional duress in some area of his or her life after a session does not mean that renewal did not occur in the specific place where ministry was administered. The ministry recipient must look carefully at the places where ministry was applied and evaluate whether the peace of Christ is resident in those specific places. If there is still pain in the specific memory, then either renewal did not occur or there are more lies yet to be exposed in that place.

Theophostic Prayer Ministry Guidelines

As a facilitator of this ministry...

• I will not be offering you counsel since Theophostic Prayer Ministry is not such, but rather interceding with you to God. I will be ministering with you in prayer seeking to help you discover with the guidance of the Holy Spirit, the root sources of the emotional pain in your life.

• I will keep any information that is shared with me during this ministry session in utmost confidentiality. I will not share any information without first obtaining permission from the one with whom I have ministered.

• I will avoid all forms of guided imagery and or directed visualization and seek to allow you to have a genuine renewal experience prayerfully directed by the Holy Spirit without information input on my part.

• I will not make ANY suggestions as to what I think your memory content may contain. I will avoid making suggestions about what I assume your lie-base thinking may be and thus allowing you to make this discovery yourself while relying on the Holy Spirit and through my asking NON-DIRECTIVE questions.

• I will only ask questions that are reflective of the actual memory content or other pertinent information that you alone have surfaced and avoid questions that are leading or ones that reflect my assumptions.

• I will not attempt to interpret or give explanation to ANY information you surface. Rather I will encourage you to listen and receive understanding from the Holy Spirit. I will not interpret your dreams, visions or other inner-mind realities but rather encourage you to follow any negative emotion that may be behind these realities and seek to find the true original memory source.

• I will ask NON-DIRECTIVE questions to help you discern the lies you may believe in your memories. For example, if you say, "I feel all alone and abandoned." I might ask, "Why do you feel all alone?" You may reply, "Because they all left me." I might say, "Why do you think they left you?" You might respond, "Because they hate me?" I might ask, "Why do you believe that they hate you?" You might say, "Because I am worthless and no good?" etc. I will avoid ALL suggestive questions such as, "Do you think you may have been abused?"

• I will withhold judgment about whether the content of your memory is true or false. However, I will seek to help you discover the source of your emotional pain in the context of the memory you have surfaced. I will allow you to come to your own conclusions in your own time concerning the validity of the content of your memories.

• I will not supply you with what I may think God wants you to know during the ministry session. I will keep my "words of knowledge" to myself until you have arrived at perfect peace in your memory as a result of your receiving truth from the Holy Spirit. I will defer my opinions and thinking to the Spirit of Christ, trusting Him to provide you with His truth and only use my words of insight for confirmation after you have received truth from Him.

• I will ask the Lord Jesus to help you to remember what you have the capacity to embrace and to help you discern the lies you believe which are contained in these memories. Example: "Lord Jesus, will you help [name] find the place where this emotional pain originated?" "Jesus, what is it you want [name] to know in this memory?" "Will you help [name] to discover what he believes that is causing him this emotional pain?"

• I will be careful to discern and call attention to any aspect of "truth" or visual you might receive during a ministry session which does not appear to be authentic and or Biblically consistent. Should this happen, I will encourage you to determine what is true or not and where the false information originated.

• I will make no assumption of the accuracy of any forgotten memory you may surface (that is one not consciously realized before the session), but rather will handle it with caution and care and will allow you to come to your own conclusions in your own time. I will encourage you to identify the emotional pain held in the context of whatever you remember and seek to help you discover any lies causing you emotional pain. After you have arrived at perfect peace in the memory, I will seek to help you determine what is true or not in its content as you choose.

• I will NOT share any visual pictures that come to my mind as a result of your sharing memory information with me. I will avoid this lest I implant ideas not your own into your thinking. Therefore, should your experience cause me to see images or pictures, I will keep them to myself.

• I will do my best not to hinder your renewal by inputting my personal assumptions, insight or thinking which is directive or leading in nature. I will keep my "words of knowledge" and "prophetic insight" to myself and only share this information after the Lord has brought you into perfect peace by way of His truth and intervention. My desire is that you have a genuine encounter with the Spirit of Christ. He alone is the only one who can truly release you of the emotional lie-base pain in your life.

• I will not make any diagnosis or suggestive opinion of what I think your problem or emotional mental condition may be unless I am a trained and qualified professional, skilled in making such diagnosis.

• I will be careful not to go beyond my training, expertise or abilities in ministry. I will seek to network with others who are more equipped and work under their supervision if at all possible. Should I find myself in a place beyond my knowledge and understanding I will seek to defer to others more equipped.

• I will seek to minister under spiritual authority and in a community of like-minded ministers who use these principles and be accountable to them and they to me. For I am a member of Christ's Body working in concert with others through Christ.

• I will avoid changing, augmenting or repackaging the Theophostic Principles and seek to apply the principles as they have been taught in as pure a form as possible to avoid misrepresenting this ministry and confusing the Body of Christ. Should I choose to do otherwise, I will clearly state my doing so to those with whom I minister so that they will not be mislead as to what is genuine Theophostic Prayer Ministry and what is not.

A Pre-ministry Evaluation

It is my desire to receive ministry from someone who is trained and adhering to the principles and Ministry Guidelines of Theophostic Prayer Ministry. Will you please complete this evaluation before we begin? Thank you.

Minister's name: _____ Date: _____

Ministry name: _____

City Location: _____

1. Have you been through the Basic Training Seminar, which includes watching all video sessions and having read the entire 400-plus pages of training materials? Was the Basic Training Manual you used the new revised edition published after 2005? YES [ ] NO [ ]

2. Are you using the Theophostic principles as your primary means of ministry and will you avoid using other forms or methods of counseling/ministry while ministering with me? YES [ ] NO [ ]

3. Will you be avoiding all forms of guided imagery, creative visualization, or suggestive thinking, or leading me to visualize anything that is not my own memory content or derived from my own thinking or from the Holy Spirit? Will you avoid guiding or directing the process through suggestive statements and/or leading questions? YES [ ] NO [ ]

4. Will you avoid providing your insight or thinking into the process as far as making suggestions as to what you think is going on or what you think may have happened to me in my past? YES [ ] NO [ ]

5. Will you allow the Holy Spirit to provide the truth during the ministry session I need rather than yourself? YES [ ] NO [ ]

6. To how many people have you ministered Theophostic principles where they reported significant emotional freedom using this approach? NONE [ ] 1-3 [ ] 3-5 [ ] 6-10 [ ] MORE THAN 10 [ ]

7. Have you experienced renewal yourself with this process, and are you continuing this mind renewal process as a regular practice for your life? YES [ ] NO [ ]

8. Are you under the authority and spiritual covering of a recognized ministry, church or professional organization? YES [ ] Who? _____ NO [ ]
If NO, please explain:

9. Do you have a problem with my sending in this evaluation along with a separate evaluation of what happens in the ministry session to the Theophostic Prayer Ministries home office? YES [ ] NO [ ]
If yes, please explain:

Conclusion

I first offered this information on how to administer the Theophostic principles in a Basic Training Seminar in February 1996. I was caught off guard by what I encountered. I was genuinely excited to share the seminar, with a hope that people would be excited as well. Instead, I was faced with a room full of people with their arms crossed, glaring at me as though I were peddling the latest infomercial product. That was 1996. Today there are tens of thousands of people ministering to hundreds of thousands of others who are finding peace and mind renewal all around the world. Oh, there are still people with their arms crossed, and even a few who are speaking out against what I am teaching, but the great majority of people are rejoicing with me as the Spirit of Jesus is setting the captives free.

It is my prayer that you will not be sidetracked by the few dissenters and nay sayers but will press on for your own renewal and find what God has in store for you. If the emotional pain that you are feeling in your day-to-day walk is coming from lie-based thinking, God wants you to know freedom. Many people come into renewal very quickly and experience the peace of Christ just a few moments into the ministry session. However, sometimes the process is long, laborious and excruciating. Still, the peace of God that awaits those who persevere is far beyond comparison to the difficulty of the journey.

Also know that mind renewal is a lifelong, twofold process. It is first the process of our lies being exposed and our willingness to follow our pain to its memory source and find experiential truth, and also the discipleship of diligent self-effort in being filled up with God's Word, so that the "word of Christ [may] richly dwell within you" (Col. 3:16). We must come to know God both cranially and experientially.

Completing a course of study and offering effective ministry are not always the same. I strongly encourage you to ask many questions of the one from whom you seek ministry. Do not assume that just because a person calls him- or herself a Theophostic minister (which he or she cannot legally do anyway) that the person is capable. Use good judgment, test the spirits and ask for references from others who are willing to share their own experiences with the one offering ministry. Even though there are many people worldwide facilitating Theophostic Prayer Ministry, it may be difficult to find a qualified person near you.

If you are unable to locate a qualified person, you may want to encourage those whom you know who are already doing other effective forms of ministry to become trained in the Theophostic principles. This way the ministry you receive may be from someone you already know and trust.

You can order all the training materials by calling or writing the Theophostic Ministries office or by visiting the ministry's Web site.

Theophostic Prayer Ministries

P.O. Box 489
Campbellsville, KY 42719
Phone: 270-465-3757
www.theophostic.com
e-mail: phostic@kyol.net

Endnotes

Introduction

1. Abreaction is physical and emotional pain flooding forth as a person embraces a painful memory. The person will often report physical pain in areas of the body where he or she was hurt during the traumatic event. Often the person will semi-lose conscious awareness of the present and believe that he or she is actually in the memory itself. If there is dissociation present, the person may even take on the personification of the child and act out the mannerisms of the child while experiencing the memory.

Chapter One

1. This example, as are those to follow, is *not* an isolated miracle of renewal. As of this writing, people all around the globe are practicing Theophostic Prayer Ministry and reporting the same wonderful results. Nearly one thousand people a month are presently completing the Basic Training Seminar and entering into the work. God is raising up an army to do the work of leading people to the only One who can bring true and lasting peace. God is faithful to do all He said that He would do as we work in concert with Him and release Him to minister according to His will and His ways.

2. Swanson, J. *Dictionary of Biblical Languages with Semantic Domains: Greek (New Testament).* (Oak Harbor: Logos Research Systems, 1997); *Theological dictionary of the New Testament, vol. 4* (Grand Rapids, MI: Eerdmans, 1964-c1976) p. 975; Strong, J. *Enhanced Strong's Lexicon.* (Ontario, Canada: Woodside Bible Fellowship, 1996).

3. I am not suggesting here that memorization of the Scriptures is not valid or important for it is. However, just because I have verses memorized does not assure me of any measure of true victory. The Pharisees had much of the Torah committed to memory but were void of true life.

Chapter Two

1. *Beyond Tolerable Recovery* was the name of the Basic Seminar Manual (1999) one received when he took the Basic Training Seminar in Theophostic Prayer Ministry.

2. When I use New Testament healing stories to explain different aspects of Theophostic Prayer Ministry, I am not equating physical healing with the mind renewal process that occurs in a Theophostic session. The renewal that occurs in a Theophostic Prayer Ministry session is the replacing of lies with truth, whereas physical healing is a different phenomena, based upon its own set of biblical and fundamental principles.

Chapter Three

1. Whenever you begin a sentence with the word "you" it is a good indication that you are blaming another person for your own lie-based pain.

2. In the Basic Training Seminar I call this a metamorphic lie. It is a present belief that was true during the actual event but is no longer true in the present state.

3. This is a deceptive cycle that is common in Christian circles. It teaches that when I am *defeated* by some sin I need to *confess* it, *repent* and turn from it, *adjust* my attitude, strategy and approach to dealing with it, and finally *perform* or try harder.

4. I teach on how to deal with dissociation and repression in the Advanced Theophostic Seminar. For information on attending a Basic or Advanced Seminar contact the Theophostic office at 270-465-3757 or www.theophostic.com.

5. Eating disorders have many different lie sources. This lie was simply what was behind her disorder. This issue is dealt with in the Advanced Seminars.

Chapter Four

1. Self-forgiveness is an interesting concept that lacks biblical support. Many teach that self-forgiveness is important and encourage it, yet there is no evidence that this is something that God desires we do. I have

discovered that when people receive truth from the Holy Spirit in their lie-based memories, they no longer feel a need for self-forgiveness.

2. Performance-based spirituality is any behavior or effort on my part to live out the Christian life by way of self-effort, trying harder, self-determination or works. What is often described as spiritual or Christian behavior is often nothing more than what lost persons could produce if they set their mind to it. True spiritual living is the effortless outflow of Christ in me that occurs as I am able to walk in perfect peace as a result of my mind being renewed to match my inner righteousness.

Chapter Five

1. Anorexia is a very serious condition that can be life threatening, and it should be dealt with in concert with a medical professional.

2. The opposite of this would be performance-based spirituality.

Chapter Six

1. Some people don't believe that SRA exists. I would invite these people to spend a few thousand hours in the trenches with these people, as I have over the last few years, to walk with them through their agonizing

memories, and to witness the Lord Jesus restoring them. People who lack experience in these areas of ministry are quick to come to unfounded conclusions based on opinions rather than on the sweat and tears of doing the work of ministry. I give logical evidence for SRA in the book *Keeping Your Ministry Out of Court,* which I co-authored with Dr. E. James Wilder. Even so, I seek to minister in the context of the person's reported reality not in what I may think or believe. I do not know what is true or not true when a person reports his belief about what has happened to him. However, it is in his reality and not my own that genuine healing and renewal can occur.

Chapter Seven

1. The Bible is full of examples of the necessity of praying for and encouraging one another. Here are but a few references. Encouragement: Rom. 1:12; Col. 4:8; 1 Thess. 2:11, 3:2, 5:11, 5:14; Heb. 3:13, 10:25. Prayer: Col. 1:3, 1:9, 4:3; 1 Thess. 5:25; 2 Thess. 1:11; Jas. 5:16.

2. A fellow came up with this idea from reading an older version of the Basic Seminar Manual where he incorrectly interpreted me as saying that I had received a divine revelation that I now call *Theophostic.* As far as I can tell, of all the tens of thousands who also read that manual he has been the only one to come to this conclusion (other than those who have quoted him). What I was describing

in this manual was how I developed the process and received insight into the Scriptures. There is a big difference between receiving insight into God's Word and receiving a new revelation from God. Insight I have had, divine revelation I have not.

3. Ed Smith, *Beyond Tolerable Recovery: Basic Seminar Manual* (Campbellsville, KY: Alathia Publishing, 1999), pp. 18-21.

Theophostic Prayer Ministry
Around the world

This ministry has found its way into over 120 countries around the world by word of mouth through people who have been blessed by it. Here are just a few samples of the testimonies received on a regular basis.

Ghana. Many of the cases that we pastors often handle are associated to superstition and witchcraft. But thanks to Theophostic Prayer Ministry, darkness is giving way to the light. By way of example, I helped a boy by praying and helping him through Theophostic Prayer Ministry to redeem his past. The family members were shocked to see their son, after only two weeks, being his normal self. Thank God Theophostic Prayer Ministry has come to Ghana. **Pastor Daniel A. Tetteh, Power Vision Church Int. Accra-Ghana**

South Africa. Theophostic Ministry has totally changed my life. When I look back at the struggles and healing journey of the past few years, I stand amazed. The major depression, shame, co-dependent behavior patterns, suicidal thinking, and agony are gone. I don't even remember all the details of all the memories until I look into old journals. And then it's: "Oh yes, I remember" — but there's no pain. It's so great to feel good about myself without having to find validation in others' opinions. And the more healing I experience, the more successful I am in leading other people to experiencing the same healing and freedom. **Karen, South Africa**

New Zealand. For me, being involved with TPM has been the source of incredible blessing — I had always had a vision for helping people be set free without having the faintest notion about how that was going to come about. With TPM, God has given me the tools to do just that. TPM has also had a significant effect on my own life. While I am aware that there are still numerous issues to be dealt with, God has renewed my mind in many areas to leave me feeling more secure personally and generally more functional and 'whole'. **René Sjardin, New Zealand**

Australia. We have been growing in the experience of Theophostic Prayer Ministry since late 1999 and, as we have each received deep mind renewal, the most noticeable change has been in our marriage. After 32 years, most of them filled with conflict, we now have a peace we never believed possible and can now turn any very occasional moment of strife into an opportunity for further healing that is such a miracle. We are active in ministering to people who have been emotionally wounded. TPM has made our ministry so much more effective and we regularly see people set free from emotional issues that have existed for a long time. **Stuart and Deanne, Sunshine Coast, Queensland, Australia**

England. My wife and I have been using TPM for 18 months and are operating as a lay ministry team in England under the authority of a local church and within a family of churches. We have seen "mind renewal" healing from many types of sexual and physical abuse and from trauma such as death of a spouse and suicide of a close family member. We have also seen people set free from depression and panic attacks. If someone had told us two years ago that we would be seeing miracles happening before our eyes, on a regular predictable basis, I would have laughed at them. Now, I know we should never be surprised when Jesus does what the Word said He would do. **Mike and Anne, Manchester, England**

Canada. Since 1998, when I took the original Basic and Advanced Training in TPM, I have been applying the TPM concepts I've learned, to the full-time specialized pastoral ministry I have been doing. The results have been such God-breathed emotional renewal and restoration in those whom I have had the privilege of ministering to — as well as in me, and my family — that I have enjoyed watching the past 6 years of prayer ministry just zoom by. **David, B.Sc., M.S.W., Ordained - C.F.C.M, Pastoral Prayer Ministry, Kitchener, Ontario, Canada**

More reports from those who have benefited

Mom in Texas thankful for kids' "REAL-LIFE relationship with their Lord"...

Mom recently I ministered to my nine year-old daughter who was "freaking out" about a regional spelling contest she was about to compete in. Three days before the event she finally broke down sobbing, confessing her fear and dread of the event. She refused to compete (even though she had earned the opportunity through a previous victory) and was begging me to pull her out of the contest and let the alternate candidate go in her place. Nothing I said could change her mind. But after 45 minutes of TPM the Lord brought her peace and calm about the event, and she was able to compete in a relaxed frame of mind and did very well. Wow! It's absolutely incredible to see my kids (7 and 9) developing a powerful, trusting, REAL-LIFE relationship with their Lord as they experience His great love and power through TPM. Thank you for bringing TPM to the everyday layperson. **Mary**

TPM blesses a ministry and a marriage.

We have found TP isn't just something you learn or are trained for but TP becomes a part of your daily lives. We are facilitator's for TPM Basic's in our small group at our church and also, see individuals by appointments. We have seen TPM redefine the healing ministry...We still need to meditate on the word daily, but Jesus is willing and ready to come to us and let us experience Him and bring renewal to our minds. We pray with numerous young people that are full of anger and rage. It is so wonderful to see them, by their wills, release their anger and Jesus meet them with His love and renew their minds…To see someone set free in this area after a lifetime of anger, resentment, bitterness, etc. and ready to receive and give love is a true work of Christ.

TPM ministry also enhances the saying "The family that prays together, stays together". Before TPM, if I got my feelings hurt or offended I would share it with my husband and he would shake it off as not a big deal that hurt more or he would pick up my hurt and be offended too. With TP the first thing my husband asks me is "how did that make you feel"? If I share with him, the second question he asks me is, do you want to pray about this? If I answer yes, I go to the feelings… We identify the lie based thinking and JESUS shows up to renew my mind and my husband and we are drawn closer together with the experience of Jesus' love and don't experience anger anymore. **Sharon**

Free from the anger for over five years…
"I had struggled with anger for all of my life. At the slightest provocation I would feel this extreme anger. When the anger would subside I would be sorry, but was helpless to stop it from overwhelming me the next time. Five years ago, at the age of 40, I went through several sessions of Theophostic Prayer Ministry, mainly focused on the sexual abuse I received as a child. Suddenly I noticed that my rage was gone! The angry thoughts and feelings are not there trying to get out and hurt someone, instead there's peace!!! <u>I received this ministry five years ago and the anger has not returned.</u> I am so thankful to the Lord for His healing, and so is my family." **Ann**

Read more reports by visiting www.theophostic.com.

Do you want to learn more about Theophostic Prayer Ministry?

Theophostic Prayer Ministry Basic Training Seminar (DVD/VHS)

This is where you begin your training in using this ministry approach to helping emotionally hurting people. There are seven training sessions (on DVD or VHS), a comprehensive 400 page seminar manual, seminar student workbook, facilitator's guide and a copy of this book "Healing Life's Hurts." The basic seminar manual and student workbooks can be ordered in quantity to allow for a training group to use the same video/DVD sessions.

Level I Advanced Training Seminar (VHS only)

Review of the Foundational Principles and Dealing with Pain-managing and Other Lie-based Behaviors. Six video-tapes and comprehensive seminar manual. Requirements for training: Must have completed the

Basic Training Seminar, administered the TPM process a minimum of 30 session hours in actual ministry setting, received a minimum of 10 hours of personal ministry from someone trained in TPM Basic Training.

Keeping Your Ministry Out of Court: Avoiding Unnecessary Litigation While Ministering to Emotionally Wounded People.

Ed M. Smith and E. James Wilder offer a means by which ministers and coun-selors can answer God's call and offer care to the emotionally wounded person while being "wise as serpents" and avoiding unnecessary litigation. This book is filled with helpful strategies for providing quality ministry and avoiding unnecessary conflict.

Facilitator's Ministry Session Flip Chart.

A "desktop" full- color flip chart presentation of all the primary principles of Theophostic Ministry to include; the basic principles, demonization, purpose of memory, dissociation and repression, and more. This tool is to be used in the actual ministry session to better educate the ministry recipient in Theophostic Ministry.

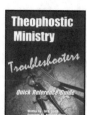

Troubleshooter's Guide to Theophostic Ministry.

This tool is a comprehensive guide to the many questions often asked. It is presented in a "If this happens... try this" format. It has a comprehensive index and table of contents for easy access of information.

Order these items today from www.theophostic.com or by calling 270-465-3757 9 am to 5 pm, M-F EST.